CAMEOS

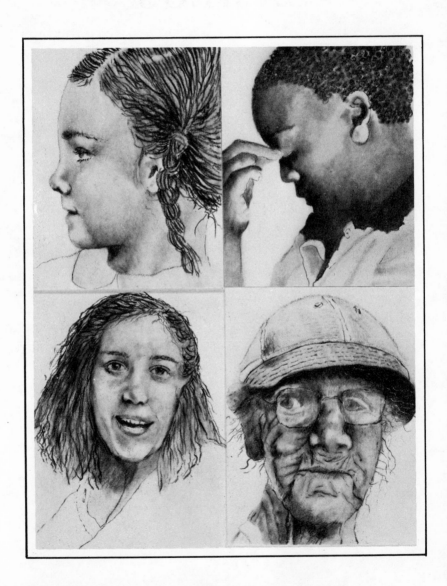

CAMEOS

12 SMALL PRESS WOMEN POETS

EDITED BY FELICE NEWMAN

THE CROSSING PRESS
Trumansburg, New York 14886

Copyright © The Crossing Press, 1978
The Crossing Press Series of Contemporary Anthologies
Front Cover & Book Design—Gini May
Back Cover & Title Page Spread—Mary A. Scott
Printed in the U.S.A.

Library of Congress Cataloging in Publication Data
Cameos: 12 Small Press Women Poets.

   (The Crossing Press series of contemporary anthologies)
   Bibliography: p.
   1. American poetry—Women authors.   2. American
poetry--20th century.   I. Newman, Felice.
PS589.C3   811'.5'408   78-16033
ISBN 0-89594-010-8
ISBN 0-89594-011-6 pbk.

This project is supported by a grant from the National Endowment
for the Arts in Washington, D.C., a Federal agency.

CONTENTS

FELICE NEWMAN
INTRODUCTION

> *The sea comes in and goes out,*
> *comes in and goes out,*
> *the sea moves with silence*
> *or with great noise*
> *against the rock-locked*
> *land I am. I am.*

> —Elizabeth Keeler
> *Of Generations And Being Woman*

The sea comes in and goes out. Cameos, carved from
the sea, are brief appearances -- of women known and
unknown, pastoral scenes and Medusa's heads -- meticu-
lously detailed in layered shell. They are familiar profiles,
often worn on the body. Because they are most often
found on a woman's body, they are viewed as a "femi-
nine" artform, "merely decorative," and thus not "pure"
art -- like her needlework and poetry.

The cameo is a miniature sculpture, as are all forms in
relief, and may depict legends and myths. They may be

1

passed among the women in a family for generations.

The cameo of a life, then, would be a delicately textured sample of that life's work, perhaps revealing the complexity of forces -- external and internal -- that produced it.

These are cameos -- of the work of twelve small press women poets. It is no coincidence that a few of these "new" poets are by no means young; they have lived a large part of their lives without serious critical consideration.

Without critical affirmation, many of us cease to write. Or, we censor ourselves, sifting from the accumulated details of our lives those events we think "safe" enough to preserve. Mary Winfrey, whose stirring historical poetry first caught my attention, is only now beginning to write in the first person -- with the support of her workshop at the Los Angeles Woman's Building. "These poems are a new genre for me, autobiographical... in fact, I'm actually writing about my daughters, and quite openly -- I wasn't sure how such poetry would be received -- but Holly Prado (workshop instructor) assured me that 'women want this kind of writing...' " (2/26/77).

Support necessitates community. We find that our private acts, our private writings, are within the context of a network which is quite public. For some this may simply be the availability of literature which influences their work. Or, community may be familial -- Maxine Shaw cites her grandmother, an unpublished writer, as an early source of encouragement, and Rachel Maines enjoys the on-going support of her mother, who is a novelist. Others, like Kate Ellen Braverman, are strongly allied with a regional writing community, working to critique and promote each other's poetry.

The point is that small press poets are energetically responding to the lack of critical consideration afforded them by the large commercial presses (themselves often subsidiaries of multi-national corporations) which publish little poetry.

Perhaps the most dramatic response is that of the feminist movement, which has come full circle in supporting a large and diverse writing network, including feminist magazines and literary journals, mail order distributors and bookstores, book publishing collectives, printers and even a women writers' institute.

The intricate process of "coming to consciousness" of a woman writer is as much a part of her stylistic growth as is her technical development. Beverly Tanenhaus, who founded the Women's Writing Workshops at Hartwick College, says, "...I refuse to write another victim poem because I no longer am a victim," and Jan Clausen, an editor of *Conditions,* a journal emphasizing lesbian literature, is among a community of lesbian writers struggling to articulate the synthesis of their political and poetic presence.

Even the phrases we need to describe ourselves are lacking. "You start out being someone's 'child', a 'sister', 'student', 'friend', 'wife', 'mother'...and one day you wake up and your label is lost in the sheets and you are swimming around inside a stranger..." (Susan North). Sometimes our poetry is the act of transcending a hostile language, which has censored our love for other women:

> no words, you say
>
> we slip
> through the nets
> of speech
>
> *mother, lover, friend*
>
> — Jan Clausen, *The Kitchen Window*

We place ourselves in settings -- the midwest, Quebec, the Orient...Virginia Gilbert's dying city (*Leaving, The Sepulchre City*) is an emotional backdrop whose violence Gilbert must observe and record. An elderly woman in a nursing home describes the scene of her dream, where she danced before a stunned audience only to wake to the "snoring shape beside her" and the factory whistle -- Dona Stein's *Visiting M. At The Happy Valley Nursing Home* superimposes these settings on the reader, the layering of the places where an elderly woman has been. We locate our pain:

> Two women who love a man who died
> We are the ground covering now
> spreading over this place   in peace
> our roots like fingers soak up tears
> three feet apart   blinking in the windy sunlight
> I lose focus
> it is minutes or decades
> since we planted you here
> we always stretch to this edge and pull back.

— Miriam Dyak, from *Dying*

Each of the poets in this book is both witness and al-
chemist, involved in an intricate process of discovery
through language. As with Alexandra Grilikhes' discovery of the female deity, we find "all transformative
powers...reside in us and it is our choice and our need to
use them well."

Felice Newman
Pittsburgh 1977

4

MARY WINFREY

I grew up in the midwest: climbing trees, swimming,
writing poetry. My parents didn't care how many rivers I
swam in as long as I made good grades in school. My
father took me to see performances of Shakespeare and
one production of Browning's *The Ring and the Book*
long before I was ten years old. He believed I would
develop a taste for blank verse, but what I actually remembered was Lady Macbeth and Cleopatra and Cordelia.
They were my first role models.

The high point of childhood, beyond learning how to
do a back jack-knife dive from a 3 meter board, was hearing Edna St. Vincent Millay read her poetry at the old
English theatre in Indianapolis. I remember she wore a
flowing wine-colored dress and her hair was long and
loose, her voice rather deep. She was what I wanted to
become some day, I knew that immediately. I said as
much to my mother who kept sending my poems to magazines; some of them actually got published. This meant
very little to me since, although I wanted to become a
poet, I also wanted to train for the Olympics and swim and
dive my way around the world. Whenever I was not swimming or writing, I memorized stanzas by Edna St. Vincent
Millay; discovered Sara Teasdale and Elinor Wylie and
H.D.; reflected on Amy Lowell. Male poets simply didn't

exist for me yet.

In college one sultry summer I heard Muriel Rukeyser read her poetry and another role model was added to my list. But I was still trying to pattern my life on Edna St. Millay, no matter what, and the effort took me to New York City, and later, to graduate school. It should have been Vassar, of course, but in actuality it turned out to be the University of Wisconsin. My experiences there did not resemble Millay's at Vassar in any way whatsoever. The university was intensely intellectual and exhaustingly male. I was compelled to write papers about Poe's esthetics, Twain's frontier spirit, Hawthorne's puritanism. Most professors would not admit that women could be good writers. I heard Aphra Behn's name ridiculed, apparently its very syllables were enough to suggest laughter. Women like Mary Wilkins Freeman and Rebecca Harding Davis, even Edith Wharton, were ignored. The only woman poet I can actually remember hearing about was Emily Dickinson, who, of course, had long ago established herself on my secret list. But she was a recluse, or very nearly one, and difficult to use as a role model when I had to face professors and students every day. I also had to choose a subject for a dissertation.

I decided to write about Zona Gale, a Wisconsin writer who had won a Pulitzer Prize for drama in 1921. I had access to her early manuscripts, letters, and "memorabilia" in the university library, almost all of it untouched. The more I learned about Zona Gale the more interested I became in her. But then my major professor declared the subject I had chosen "frail and insubstantial". He doubted whether Zona Gale could carry the full weight of the doctorate. Soon afterwards I left graduate school, taught for a while and got married.

Many years later, after my three daughters were born and I was living in California, I found a scholarly study of Zona Gale on the library shelves. It had been written by a man at the University of Oregon! However, by this time I knew I was a feminist; and I was reading the poems in my notebook aloud to other women and studying all the notes I had ever taken. Because I had files on women and history, mythological women, queens and visionaries...

notes that had been no use to me in colleges. Suddenly I discovered women poets everywhere; and I read them and met them, as many as I could. They were all different and remarkable.

Yet there was still only one who had a name that was a poem in itself. I used to chant this name, close my eyes and see the long purple gown, the swinging hair. It was an act of love. It still is.

Kleis

listen   listen
the vast centuries raise a mound
a death barrow of hate and darkness
bone and weed mingle with pure ware
deliberately smashed   tiny fragments of song

listen   listen

across that ugly barricade
a few lines of music dance
the rustling night wind breathes a message
the apple swings at the top of its branch
a soft mouth praises "the golden flower
for whom I would not give all Lydia or lovely Lesbos"

listen   listen

Sappho
cradles
her daughter

thoughts about Clara Schumann

who
years after
the discipline   the concerts   the performances   the applause
is a paragraph in an encyclopedia: wife   pianist
is a handclasp in her husbands music   the borrowed themes
woven through Roberts tapestries that banner the length of Europe
Clara completely used up, you would think, by the business of giving
consolations and martyrdoms
in a word, subsumed

not at all
theres a Clara who stays light and contained
a solitary devising what she loves most: songs   impromptus
a polonaise   mazurkas   variations
why, along
one small space on the horizon
you may observe Brahms dwindle   disappear in his own mirror
protesting no woman could ever write the concerto
she wrote at sixteen

alive
the concerto itself
breaks loose
leaps   falls and unwinds bright labyrinths
and pools of sound so unexpected   you could ask
is this the
true dimension then   Clara travelling the length of her music?
after the concerto
where are the songs   the variations, yes
where are the others?

Gertrude Ederle swims the Channel
      (August 6, 1926)

waves are hard
the swimmers arms and mouth
stitch bubbles through stone
                  reach across cobbled currents
                        mountain to slope to cavern
each must be gotten through
while a brass bull tide hammers the head bones blue
the swimmers feet pound back

on the over lap   the uneasy angle
where sky and water tilt
boats go by
they bend, men hang down and call *come out   come out*
the swimmers mouth shapes a musical phrase
what for? she sings into the seas snout
into the worlds eye

waves are feathering wings
to speed the swimmer   as she emerges
no goddess served on a half shell
but a woman rolled in a burst of oil and shingle
her goggles smeared   bruised   cold
above all cold
she leaves the sea
and the men who pine for an Aphrodite stare
who is she?
why does she swim or paint or sail or write or dare
any of these avalanches? their hesitation
stumbles along the sand   tugs at the question
she herself answers
with her thrusting thunders
                    her broken ear drums
                              her exultation

hera of the locker room

its almost a dream   she says
or a chapter from a story book   and as she begins talking
the women allow a frost to
edge through the locker room
the women are young and in a hurry
they wish this angular old swimmer
could choose some other hour
to reminisce
still, they listen   and hear
words that drift and explode
like fireworks spangling
the cool metal silence

lets put it different she says
maybe more formal   since ive
got an announcement to make   imagine
me   what i did yesterday   me after
years and years dreaming about it and
only a little practice in between kids
so to speak   and jobs   why honestly
i really did win first place swimming
backstroke in the city competition   won a
medal i did   me   an athlete   imagine
because i guess you can tell easy enough
i just turned fifty-six

the swimmers neck is bent
white hair mantling the forehead
she cannot see what the women see:
a swift blazing enchantment
the sudden glimpse of the goddess
shining through muscle and vein
indestructible, casual in her strength

the conditioning

she explains

i used to do surface dives
           bending at the waist, a quick slashing thrust
           toes pointing, no displacement of the water, a
           long sweep through heavy green rhythm, the final
           arching and pulling into sunlight, the top of the sea

and so these days when i open
           and close doors, slice grapefruit and push
           dials slowly rotating to the left   one
           motion following another like wet footprints
           when the faucet jerks and foams for the hundredth time

why, i am aware
           of the position of muscle and bone, the sliding
           pistons and wheels inside me, the curve
           on the oven door   my steel face saying yes
           it is its me its really me and my years
           years old old old habits habits habits habits

historical footnote

the early burghers of Florence   persuading the churchmen
to instruct women to stop wearing wool since wool can be
sold more profitably in other, better markets   say

at the beginning   my lords   touch upon virtue, the joy
of frugality   not giving   but giving up
define modesty   to be satisfied with a little
sacking   good plain stuff worn over the body
and if virtue does not avail   my lords   women being
as they are wasteful and vain   remind them

how once a snake got into them, they let a snake enter
and the hair   they must cover it   cover   be covered
by husbands   wives   obey your husbands   women
obey
wives o
be covered
obey
or
be
burned

Charlotte Corday / Marat
(July 13, 1793)

the country girl in Paris
rises early   pulls on white gloves   carries a fan of green paper
she moves to a distant rhythm she has memorized
harboring her skirts from the soot on apartment walls
she does not even bother to sharpen the knife

the citizen
calls himself the rage of the people
his hands hunger   he festers
he flattens imaginary grapes insisting they are heads
and must go to the guillotine as soon as he finishes writing
he has no use for women of her sort   the tight-knit kind

she says she brings names to fatten his lists   good, he says
every name goes to feed the guillotine tomorrow
but then the pen he is using streaks off the page
the act that enfolds them takes less time than love
yet keeps them inseparable   they fuse
binding each other's gaze in a fixed stare
a sour future which she accepts with a shrug
she consecrates the proud body   the Norman head

she wears the red chemise of the murderer like a toga
keeping severe and taut on the ride to the guillotine
her death looks exactly as she intends it to look

what else does she intend, this provincial activist
with a conscience as transparent as a pane of glass?
why, to end one revolution and start another
she would gladly prepare a list beginning Abraham
Alaric, Alexander, Allah, Beria, Bismark
Bonaparte, Charles, Constantine, Darius, Edward
Ferdinand, Genghis, Hitler --
these are the names you live and die by (she reads)
you take your chance with them
I took mine

at the diagnostician's office

i am glad you mention
while mononucleosis is my favorite disease   the doctor smiles
not unlike typhoid   i am speaking of origins and traces
that led us to typhoid mary   the nuclear source
halfway around the world infecting thousands possibly all
the sailors in port and just exactly
my current thesis points to a mono mary
as carrier   not altogether proven of course   not yet
the friendly doctor's eyes
close like nutcrackers above the raffia heads from yukatan
the photographs of his daughters crouching on horseback
at the last hurdle   his myth framed in
cancer   the black death erysipelas   gifts from
pandora's inexhaustible box
traced through small talk and humor and very likely
the doctor's daughters too   oh
very likely   he concludes nodding with pleasure
oh very likely   very like

meeting

i find
women can slip
from the pages of a book
just like pressed flowers
they drop singly or in sprays
transparency of queen anne's lace
orange tiger lily tough

and once i found
blooming at the center of a page
flickering through the mediaeval dampness
the odd exquisite
sophonisba anguissola
who painted portraits
who taught men how to paint
when she herself was blind

for a moment
i touch hyacinths   i feel
the brush stroke of petals
on my cheek

at menopause

my body is the grapevine that grows and lengthens
kinked rope trained to obey each season
but ripening comes to a stop
the twigs slant without fruit
no purple triangles   juices bursting rich skins
(the seasons turn over, the harvesting ends)

my body's sinews are building a cautious arbor
its thick leaves shade the sun
people shelter beneath like birds   my roots send
fine nerves into the soil to lengthen
never has earth nourished me more
(the seasons turn over, the fragrances blend)

Demeter's Song

Korė is back, my daughter returns
the rapist sleeps
in his gutted lands
through dead men the narcissis vaults and the wheat
and my child walks triumphant
Korė, oh Korė   give me your hands!

MIRIAM DYAK

Once there was a young woman who worked in an alphabet factory and went to a therapist every Thursday at 5:15. She told him how she was terrified of her own face in the mirror, she could never get enough air into her lungs, how she wanted to be a Poet with a capital P. She compared herself to everyone but her own "multidimensional soul" and she never compared favorably. She had not learned to say she lacked harmony, peace, her own sense of purpose. Then came the Women's Movement, friendships with other poets, meditation, a slowly gathering strength.

I am looking for unity. Writing, building a house, the garden, astrology, working with other women, bartering yoga lessons for home-baked bread, painting with my eyes orange, raveling and expanding dreams, counseling, traveling to work and beyond -- this is how I live and it all has to work together symbolically and physically for my life to have meaning, to pattern itself into art, to mesh that pattern with the World. And the World is the 21st card in the deck, my destiny number, the woman risen to cosmic awareness, the true androgyne.

I no longer want to be a Poet. I work with energy, the most basic, simple, dynamic, undefinable element. I want to be there again and again at the center of that electric leap where energy transforms into life. I am both a witness and a catalyst. It happens most intensely and most often for me in the private act of writing poems -- in the essential energy form of images within the structures of poems. It happens again sometimes in reading poems to others, often in meditation, tangibly in sending healing through my hands, dramatically in gestalt work. It is the "one-pointedness" of yoga when all else is forgotten and I am simply there. It is my whole body stretching with the garden in spring, mixing herbs, saying blessings, dancing under the high sun. And in winter when I will my feet to go lightly over the snow and follow the rabbit's long tracks.

The poetic intensity persists through the light and dark of living. The *Dying* poems come from a time when one of our communal family was dying of cancer. None of us had ever been deeply involved in the process of dying. We believed and disbelieved what was happening to us. We fought against it; and then when we began to accept it, we fought the medical system which is set up more to fight the process of death and dying than to aid in the process of the whole life cycle. The concept of life cycles is more Eastern, wholistic, feminist, definitely anti-science, anti-church, anti-american, anti-patriarchy, anti-death. We continually discover that our most basic life processes are intensely political.

Dying grew out of a journal of notes and images I kept during the months he was dying. As a writer, they were my instinctive outlet, my way to keep head above water; but they were also a conscious expression of creation, a protest against destruction. I had to realize that I do not lose my artist's perspective no matter how catastrophic the life around me becomes; and that rather than indulge in guilt over "using" sickness for poetry, it is my job to express the creative energy in all I perceive. At one point I told him that I was writing about what was happening to him and asked him how he felt about it. He said, "but you always write poems, that's what you do."

My first book of poems, *Fire Under Water,* (New Victoria Publishers) grew out of my relationship with my mother, myself, with other women and with men. Now

we are building a house and my poems are growing out
of the metaphor of building -- physically and spiritually.
I have no definite plans -- I plant and wait and see how
things grow.

On Having To Go Round The Circle And State Our Philosophies

I really don't want to say anymore
what you want to hear
I want to say: I am a person
who refuses to make a multiple choice
who scribbles in   over 1 to 5
most/least   strongly   (dis) & agree
who refuses to see anything
as less than cosmic

  Whole galaxies of sisterhood
  dribble into chronic complaint
  the milky way streams
  streaking dust through our finger bones
  as we knit our intricate pain
  our swollen desire

I want to be: ULTIMATELY RESPONSIBLE
My life is a gem stone
breaking through anthracite
My life is a spider weaving our cycles
even when you step down
the center body stays hard and shining
a black coin
After all this is dead   you will know me

January 23, 1976

the axe

if I hear you
say my body is softer than yours
and you   a woman   arc over me
in a rainbow of muscle
then your voice runs across my arms like strings
the blade bounces and hits back

if I think about your presence
see you run to leap the roof
in one bound
my attention wavers   the blade
thuds down at an angle and sticks

when my eyes are empty as lightning rods
I see the wood fly apart twice
once before   once after   it happens
the blade swings weightlessly to the ground

Winter Solstice 1975

26° below zero   the cats fly
up walls   burn
their paws on the stove
all the glass breaks   festival of icecolors
lemon juice   windex   syrup   explode
Alone   I live in the oven
suck the pen to make it flow
voices from Florida bubble out the phone
a frozen foam of sound still hangs in the air
The bed swallows   anything that comes near it
I stand in front of the mirror   count to 60
wait   for my face to disappear

April 6

This endless beginning
nothing will move forward
April and the snow spreads out again
over the first mud
I come here rarely
the harvesters drag out half the pines
and it is more unfamiliar
They are careful with their crawler
snailing through the wet   trailing the browncut logs behind
deer stay at a distance
an uneasy peace waiting change

List:
dig 2 holes 6 ft deep to test for drainage
mark the trees with yellow so we can clear
for a house and road
call the man about the well
talk to the man about windmills
think about where to plant the squash

in the body cells impatience swells like spring seed
every night I itch   dream of breaking through
I wake with my teeth clenched

Three

I.

three mouths
                kiss
        like fish   fan out
                                for the dance
we dive
        with no water
                hands and tongues
                        tread
        the knobby   succulent   kelp

II.

there is no reason
for our ecstasy -
                it gentles us
                                away
from locked arms
        gestures of drowning
it holds us up
        the smiling mirror
                        to our play

III.

the sign   of blessing
        from the Mother
                                is a doe
                                        flying
        over the blackberries
as we drive
                through the dark   tree tunnels
                                all the way home

Forbidden Sweets

6 percent   of the world's population
consumes 60 percent of all resources
and stays slim
On the subway my mother and father
hate the fat   point
each one out to me   a miracle of failure
broken covenant of Amerika
better to gorge and eat your own long white fingers
so it all spew out   unused   unusable
better to eat our dark children
secret sweets   forbidden   Welcome!
to the private feast   the delicate ladies
who never eat in public
will stuff themselves on the back stairs
while talking charity and Planned Parenthood
let the poor have cake and starch and chemical colas
    "How could anyone allow
    themselves to get that way?
    It's fantastic   really fantastic!
    You'd think she was pregnant
    if she weren't so old."
carrying out guilt   like an enormous baby
somebody has to

*

better to gorge and eat your own long white fingers
so it all spews out   unused   unusable

Now the Golden Society splits open   like a seam
the fat ooze out   cream puff filling   spilling
over becoming
                the gray   we walk on
                the candy wrapper
                our daily trash

from **Dying**

XVI

After a night of whippoorwills
and dreams good enough to turn back to
the morning sun sucks up the dew
daisies   iris   apple flower
look in at the window
cracked wheat steams into our nostrils
joy runs in and out through my skin

I take your hand and show you the colors
today   I am a plump hospital nurse
    "You will take a walk. No question.
        You are going to get some air! some sun!"
I feel strong in the buoyancy of light and dreams
I could carry you down to the road over the water to another life!

XXIII

You are a troll
you hobble towards us
smelling of roots and compost
of animal life   already
turned back to the earth

We embrace we four
but you are no longer human
you have grown dark and magical
                    twisted and dying
dying falling dying falling
down through the ground

XXVII

The garden   at last
begins to yield
   a few beans
   salad
   skinny squash
it's been a bad summer
   too much rain
   too much quack grass
   and slugs
In a way
it's you we are eating
with the lettuce and the stunted peas

This is the summer of your dying
we have denied it a thousand times
we have stared into it
as numbly as frogs into light
we have smiled and ached and held
   our broken faces
but   we have tended it carefully
all the same

We have watered and weeded
we have sprayed toxins
we have said prayers
we have fed it bone and blood

so that now   I know
with the sharp herbs
the radishes   the green rocket
it is you   at last
we are eating
it is you we are turning to mulch
for the fall
already I sense you
lying out under the bean poles
your words hovering
over new snow

XXXIX

We tie up the world around you
parcel you off to your corner
your 18 square feet of ground and grass
across from the schoolyard   in the village
where the poor stay on after death

I am efficient
I buy and sell
I call on the phone   men
who will pick up and deliver
    your body
    your money
    your tools

and when I come home
I am astonished
you are not yet dead

XLI

I saw your coffin today
a friend made it
it is enormous
I thought I would vomit
I thought my sweat would turn black
I thought there was an iron nail in my stomach
But it was only a box made of pine
and a workshop filled with kind faces

XLIII

Last night I dreamed
we put you in the toybox
and piled all the books in around you
you lay calmly   and didn't move an inch

We each kissed you
one last time before sleep
then we nailed down the lid
and dropped you into the snow
deep and layered   like quilts

XLIX

november 28

so today finally I was no longer waiting
I touched death at the top of the stairs like a dog
it was so familiar
I walked into your room at noon
to see if you were hungry
to see if you were sleeping
to see if I could leave you for a minute
to see if you were frightened   crying   dreaming

I found you gone from your body
you left it cold and quiet in the bed   like snow
sometime in the morning you left it
alone   asleep   you died
while I was in the kitchen typing poems
at the last you had no need

L

"I always compare you to a drifting log with iron nails in it.
Let my brother float in, in that way.
Let him float ashore on a good sandy beach."
    (The Mourning Song of Small-Lake-Underneath)

We gathered the things you would want
and placed them carefully around you
    pictures   tools   bowls   poems
    your wandering jew and the teddy bear at your head
    shoes   shirts   pants   at your feet
    your wallet   the I Ching

it was a small room   a shrine
when we were done
your head lay on the yellow-flowered pillow
old quilts and blankets and sheepskin wrapping you
you looked at once like a tiny child and an old man

At home we played Bach all night for you

In the morning early we took shovels
eight women and three men
and dug the still soft earth for your grave
the sun was like clear water
and the dog ran crazy as spring
through the stones

They brought you in a fancy car
according to the law
with curtains and a white-faced man   aping death
we took you from them   laid you down
made a circle   silent   around you
letting our tears run down with the sunlight
letting our ache sink into the earth

We set a rock from the old stone wall at your head

LI

April 30, 1975

Moving backwards suddenly
we come to the edge of our lives
violas   purple   yellow   white
bloom from your body
before even the grass takes color
The earth has sunk another inch
in this small gravegarden
we marvel   leaning over your death

Two women who love a man who died
we are the ground covering now
spreading over this place in peace
our roots like fingers soak up tears
three feet apart   blinking in the windy sunlight
I lose focus
it is minutes or decades
since we planted you here
we always stretch to this edge and pull back

It is true some things are easier
I can move to her   we touch   our bones soften
We have land now   a garden
It swells to 30 acres and draws back to this spot again
slowly the holes sink and fill

BEVERLY TANENHAUS

I am trying to define myself as a woman-identified woman. This means liberating myself from the obsessive male escort applaud by most magazines, TV shows, and grandparents; most importantly, it means retrieving consciousness of the value of women's experience. In my life, I feel I've been able to work out my own definitions, to gradually extricate myself from the bonanza of male approval and to acknowledge deeply the importance of my friendships with women. I am waiting for this new consciousness to surface in my poems. Shyness, the lack of traditional language familiar to these experiences, a lifetime training that has trivialized female experience make it more difficult to record these women happenings than, let's say, a flamboyantly destructive love affair with a man. But I refuse to write another victim poem because I no longer am a victim; I'm willing to give up a literary genre that I was getting rather good at, a cultivated expertise in documenting helplessness. Instead, I'm excited about developing new techniques, metaphors, retrieving details that now count, to joyfully record the reunion with my sisters and the flourishing of self-love. As a person who feels degraded daily by the media where too many of us are compulsively brushing with Ultra-Brite in between beaming over cake

mix successes, I eagerly wait for, receive the literature
of women, by women that restores our dignity and strength.
Our lives depend on this.

Quasi-Liberation In Upstate New York

You overhear conversations in the street.
Children you've never noticed
Suddenly appear with their toys.
You realize you live in a neighborhood
Where small town friendliness is not a fact.
You know no one in these houses,
Although you've memorized the colors of their cars
And share with them each morning and evening
The sound of bells.

You comfort yourself with the leaves of trees
Outside your window, the delicate greens
Crowding for your attention; the telephone poles
Gallantly function as landmarks, your neighbor's porch
Becomes a souvenir.
You understand the change of seasons
By the arrival and departure of wicker chairs,
The heavy snow shovel leaning against bags of salt,
Colored corn hung cross-wise over the door --
Old gesture of hospitality evolved into
Decoration.

When the dogs bark
You pretend it's a coded message meant for you
Less obvious than the drum,
More accurate than smoke, drifting between hills.

"I thought an old lady lived upstairs!"
After eight months the mailman has noticed you,
Surprised by your twenty-five years.

Quickly you review the valentines,
The letters from your friends, the copies
Of *MS.* magazine and decide that no, he
Is wrong

You are not old; you are simply
The lady upstairs, Rapunzel trapped
Inside a small apartment, self-sufficient
And employed

Making it in your own way
In a little town where
The ice cream flavors haven't
Changed in twenty years,
Where a family will stand watch all day,
Grieving, as the county's saws cut down
The elm trees out in front

Where you float leaves
In a jar on the window sill
Tempting new roots
To get by.

First you tell him all your problems.

The lake is ravenous.
It appropriates the shore.
This makes it possible for you to
Drown several times a day.
The water is cold and thick with mud.
You are afraid of fish.

He is not impressed.
He knows you well.
You are prone to exaggeration.
He can calculate the boundings
Of your tongue.
He trips you up.

Thank him for his honesty.
Make him dinner.
He appreciates your thoughtfulness.
You have included
His favorite dessert.

The next day
At dinnertime he kisses you.
Your cheek is branded; you are his.
You wonder if everyone
Can see the mark or
Are you the only one
Who understands the bargain.
The mirror gives you an answer.
You are grateful that the cheap terms
Are your secret.

Again,
He asks about your day.
You tell him you are not happy.

The trees will not speak to you.
The grass is exclusive.
Only the stones will allow you to hold them.
They are like mute amputees in your hand.
You have no friends.

He listens carefully.
He can measure anguish.
You do not qualify.
Faker! Faker!
You do not deserve his sympathy.
You are not old, you are not ailing,
You have no dead.
You are untested and
Whimper at extraneous disaster.

He is warning you.
He has real troubles of his own.
For him, you exist as magic.

Do not disappoint him.
Sing, tell stories to his fingers,
Devise a beauty contest for his toes.

Call his chest an ocean,
His hair feathered seaweeds,
His eyes two blue shells
That chant your name so softly.

Choose your betrayal.

Do not cry.
This is not music.

You understand your responsibilities.
You have chosen your betrayal.
Now succeed in making good.

He cannot understand you.
You interrupt his dinner.
Do not cry.
You are alarming him.
You will lose him.

He surmises the situation.
You need affection.
Gallantly, he leads you to the bedroom.

He will smash you on his rocks.

My Hair Is Black

Yesterday you were kind, a new breed
Of man I would believe in; your beard
A fringe of welcome to your lips,
Your tongue asking no questions
I could not answer.

You, the rabbi,
Explaining why the women
Should not cut their hair
To please the men in prayer shawls.

This was a sacrifice
Unnecessary to understand the Torah,
A brutal route to God.

Last night I dreamed I was running towards you
Slowly black feathers floated behind me   Black feathers
Mounding my footsteps   Black feathers

How easily you become the enemy.
How ugly I look without my hair.

I.

She tells you she is beautiful.
Her words are delicacies on a silver tray.
Deftly, the handles turn in on themselves.
The polished knots reflect the light.

You want to believe her.
You want to eat the food of angels.
You are tired of meat and water,
Of basic survival.

You deserve a bounty
To scallop your boredom
To compete with your pain
To make your life more interesting.

You think you will try her.

Easily, she talks to you.
Her words are honey on your tongue.
Your teeth are coated.
Even your throat is a luxury.
When you swallow, you feel rewarded.

Take her home.

II.

She comes to beg. Without a tambourine, without
a wooden cane, a pencil cup, she comes to beg. Finally,
you have realized this. You see her hands, which cooked
your food and rubbed your back and wrote your checks, as
plotting your obedience.

Her fingers, mute sideshows of command, send you
messages in the dark. Even your dreams are pocked by plea.
Tentacles of silk dissect your body into squares. Easily,
you will be organized and claimed.

Substitute a dummy for yourself. Give her dust
instead of blood, stitchings for her fingertips, deadweight
for her acrobats. She will never know that you are gone.
She will call again, her hands frisking the dark, her
fingers scavenging for coins. She will collect nothing
that is yours.

Reunion

Mother
in a restaurant
you hug me
and praise my income
your daughter
making money
smiling   coming home
in a small way
a success

Despite
the bad times
we lived through
the flimsy leaves trembling
the tree
rooted
with an implacability
you called love

when I called you
a broken bowl
when I wanted
only perfect crockery
for my table
which you
and all your magazines
would beg to polish

I dreamed
I was crying
and you came to comfort me
with the pretty lozenges
you call insight

Already I had memorized
that formula from the box
a long time ago
that taste began to bore me

As I told you this
I watched your face
melting like a candle
disfigured
by a terrible fire
whose heat sickens
for a lifetime

I am responsible
I feel no guilt
There is no need to share this dream with you

Now in this restaurant
across the table
we argue about dessert
and finally agree to share
a piece of cheesecake

Our forks crisscross
Laughingly, we separate the tines

KATE ELLEN BRAVERMAN

There are many things to be said at this point. So grab a cigarette (does anyone read poetry and not smoke?) a cup of coffee and let's chat a bit.

I have to tell you something about where I'm at. And it's hard to articulate. I haven't published much in the last eight months. I have sixty poems in the mail right now at twelve different magazines. And that's just the stuff I bothered to type up. I'm half way through my third unpublished book, not chapbook books, but hundred and fifty page manuscripts, fifty or sixty long poems. God knows how many chapbooks. The "feminist" (woman/ rage -- woman/angry. . . how dare she?) is very hard to publish. The very personal poems are very hard to publish. The brand new, ten page long poems I'm doing now are *impossible* to publish.

First of all, it seems that the poems currently being published by the "name" small magazines are interchangeable. Halpern's anthology (*The American Poetry Anthology*) reads like one long poem. The currently acceptable style (The Iowa and New York style) can be loosely characterized as: Safe and middle of the road. The poems are generally short, one page. By safe, I mean that the poet is dealing with subject matter he/she already understands. *The poet is merely restating what he already knows about the world.* With this fundamental aspect in mind, the only problem is how to *freshly* restate what he already knows. This leads to academic poetry, poetry of strain, poetry that is called "experimental" but is actually mechanistic, artificial and soulless, anything but what experimental should really mean. The acceptable poem is *flawless.* It is a poem of technique and it makes no mistakes. The problem with the currently acceptable poem as I see it is that in addition to not making any mistakes, *it doesn't take any chances, it doesn't take any risks, it isn't ambitious.* Poetry must (my fundamental assumption) deal with what the poet does not yet know. *It must be a work of exploration.* The poetry of exploration, by confronting what the poet doesn't know, by taking the enormous risk of shining a flashlight into the pitch black has the advantage of stumbling on the brilliant connections that make us human. (In other words, art). I see that as Plath's greatest strength, that she stumbled on connections. That's what gives her work (to me, and I'm only talking about *Ariel*) such fantastic energy. Connections spark/sizzle/energy.

Now, I don't know how much you are or are not seeing where I'm at so far. I've basically disconnected myself from the mainstream of current poetry by operating on a fundamentally different set of principles. I've written my poems of careful restatement. I call them exercises. O.K. Once severed from the Iowa/New York mainstream, there is the problem of L.A.

L.A. poetry (if anyone thinks about it at all) is noted or called the Bukowski school. If you've read Bukowski and his disciples, certain generalizations can be made. The L.A. school deals with the superficial. The eye sees what is obviously there -- the billboards, neon, freeway nightmare. Bukowski has managed to confuse the painful problems of human self-awareness with the painful problems associated with a hangover. The substance of his art is materially generally reserved for aspirin commercials. That's the L.A. school.

(At this point, violins will please strike up a chorus of ONE AGAINST THE WORLD. . . . . . .)

There is a subschool of L.A. poetry. L.A. has always existed in artistic isolation. There are a handful of people I know who have responded to this isolation by experimenting, by exploring, by dealing with a very personal, emotional internal reality, an examination of their humanity. . . . art.

Basically we have commitment and energy, but can't define/articulate what we are doing in an academic, in a critical sense. We are too close to it? Too involved? It's been six years since I set foot in a university, and the critical tools I once had have eroded. I don't believe that we can be a movement until we define our uniqueness.

It's taken me four years to come up with the ideas in this letter and two and a half hours to write this letter. I hope I have said something of interest.

August 27, 1976

7 P.M.

It's the quality of light
that excites me.
The small safe arcs
in a herd of restless dark things
feeding on the soft edges
of the room,
in black puddles of tar
where strangers lose their bones.

It's a 7 P.M. in Hollywood yellow.
Whore yellow.   Junky yellow.
A world of old dressing tables
stained with divorce and migraines.

A bad hour for decisions.
Shadows prepare an invasion
while I run the bath.
The truth is swollen shut.
I cannot touch it,
even with my tongue.
I will always marry the wrong men.
None of them will do.
Not with surgery and therapy,
protein and new clothing.
Not tonight or next year or ever.

There are no answers in the mirror,
smoking done, putting on make-up,
pretending I'm a jazz singer
in a backstage dressing room.

This is the hour the men return
empty and dry as old milk bottles.

Weekend Man

Smoke.
A mud brown haze
of barbeques, trucks coughing,
buses pushing through fat air,
charred hotdogs, eight months
without rain.
At the core, more
smells rising with the flowers,
damaged flesh torn or burned
mixing with parched grass.

This is the edge.
The last outpost.
Land of the killer sun.
Liquid morning.
Death by melting.
Death by yellow oxygen.

The streets are squashed
miniature sets of scaled down
boxes growing in rows
like a further skin on top
of your head.
Here is your white picket fence
with square part acre to mow,
to throw your weekend shoulders
against and feel sweat,
the cool man fever.

Why are your eyes flat,
dulled grey like moths
sucked into cities
and stranded?

It is Sunday.
Leaning is permitted.
Survey your staked perimeter
with standard issue rose bushes
one pink and one red.

Here is your curse of crab grass.
And one child's toy lost,
broken and edged with rust
tossed in the thin spiked shadow
of a trimmed bush.

Can you feel your toes
grown hard and oddly flexible?
A new mutation, protection
from the drift.
You must hang on here,
inches from the sea.

Your chaise lounge is unsteady
on torn hinges. Fix it.
And polish your car.
Your belly pushes out from your belt,
your legs ache, you cough
and stare into the blank side
of the house next door.
The unread newspaper is draped
like a blanket across your lap.
You close your eyes and see
grey tangled alleys beyond
the back door.
Black wings beat inside your chest.
Think. Make a list.

Storm clouds. Crescents of red
moon. Scarecrows in fields you
have never seen. New breasts.
A man enters a deserted shack
where a pale young woman waits.

Your lips twist on polished grooves.
You take the air as if to speak.
But there is only one word.

No.

My Husband Who Is Not My Husband

My husband who is not my husband
sleeps face up,
a pale beached sea mammal
dragging air through an opening
snoring, farting with impunity.
Naked, in sunlight and old slippers
he is sniffing in my kitchen.
He will have eggs sunnyside up,
toast and peppermint tea.
(But he will not marry me.)
He is afraid his paintings won't sell.
Or that I and the small
chromosome damaged bawling morons
will grow fat from his art.
He thinks it better now
with us lean,
and the hallway so empty
you can hear old pins breathe.
He calls me girlfriend,
though I am old and plump
as a wife
and faithful.
He is uncertain.
I drink too much.
He wants me to smile more.
He says I whisper in corners
with my mother.
He is too clever.
(This is not the first time.)
My husband who is not my husband
will not even speculate
on the colors and shapes
of babies unborn,
curled on the dusty shelves
of my belly.

Details

I must remember the details.
Sunlight on the blond hairs
of your arm.
Moods changing your eyes
now grey, now blue.

Already it begins.
The blank stormy slide
into that other side.

When you know the chairs
and have worn a path
through the carpets
you will dust me off
like a prop,
tell me when to dance,
when to lie still
and shut up.

Before I must start flirting
with pills and the car exhaust
in my hunger for the dark,
the black arms
you will awaken.

Already they are scratching.
The walking death.
I am inhabited.
Small things, dwarves
or lost children
sing in my garden.
I cannot see them.
They skirt past my eyes,
a patch of fast black.
It always begins this way.

I must remember your fingers
breaking French bread
brushing the crumbs
on your pants leg.
Your profile while you cut cheese.
The knife in your hand
and your smile.

Picking Up Your Mail

Climbing the stairs
wearing blue sunglasses and a new smile,
you study one corner of the wall.
Is it familiar,
that space between my shoulder?
You painted it that color,
under duress, yes,
a parrot yellow compromise
of our last summer.
I washed brushes, woodwork,
content in my new Sistine Chapel.
Now you come to retrieve your mail.
You will refuse tea,
concentrating on your new biology,
barefoot, I am a small dark thing,
a sub-species, not reaching your chin.
Finding an inability for things mechanical,
you shrug.

Your letters are on the window sill.
Careful,
you avoid the bookcase shadows,
dark accusing glance of old titles,
lying threads of some other life.

Our backyard is a tangled garden,
a growing ruin,
the white wood fence leans into the winds,
the outdoor chairs lay
where storms have pushed them,
wounded, upended wire creatures
bleeding rust.
Detached and tense, opening letters:
Secret documents consumed on the
far side of the room,
folded and shoved into your pockets.
You're gathering momentum.

I know you want
your fingerprints back,
the drops of water from the shower.
I have encased them in glass
our life preserved, dusted
by eras and nuances of mood.
We orbit each other,
finding a final formality.
Not even our shadows collide.

Lies

You say I lay for years
in the fleshy web of your shoulder
feeding on your hot salty milk
moaning, twisted in sheet
our hips twin hills.
Lies.
Your bed is pure and unscarred
thick walls shutting out
Washington Boulevard.
Your skin is clear of indentations.
You are untouched
first generation Los Angeles
with even white teeth.

Your legacy of balanced meals
and music lessons after school.
Your fat mother in her kitchen
punctual, begging you for one
more spoon of vegetables.
Fearing your withdrawal,
temper and scorn.
You, the first born son.
Living six years above a bar.
Tending your collections
of tropical fish, pennies
in jars, parts of bicycles.
Inching into madness
in silence, by degree.
Savoring the experience.
The things that simply happen
when you can refuse nothing.
The strange women disrobing
leaving behind pieces of themselves.
A chair upholstered in velvet,
a satin vest, pressed flowers
in a coffee cup.
You say I laughed
and made gardens of window ledges.
Lies.
The window sills are empty.
The street is dulled by fog.
You, sleep well.

Job Interview

Background

Four brothers went by train
from Kiev to Antwerp.
They never met again.
The bronx was farm land.
The first born gambled
and moved to Baltimore.
That was later,
during the war.

A red haired girl worked
East Side factories at fourteen,
afraid of subways and machinery.
She had never even been
to Warsaw.
She gave birth in Ellis Island.
The daughter was made
a Ward of the State.

Childhood Illness

You will notice I checked measles.
My mother sewed red spots
on my rag doll.
It took her an entire day.

But you ask nothing about winter.
My father took me sledding
He pulled me to the top of hills.
In vacant lots we found streams.
That was in Philadelphia.

Sawtelle Boulevard (twice)

I lived on Sawtelle Boulevard
when I was eight
and the San Diego Freeway
was a harsh brown beanfield.

They said tractors were inching
south through the dirt.
But we did not believe them.

Ten years later
I returned with my husband
to precisely the same building,
the same pale undernourished palms,
pieces of courtyard, slat blinds
and long grey cement hallways
neat and dull as a checker board.

Education

In Berkeley the yards lost
their boundaries.
Yellow and purple wildflowers
spilled over sidewalks,
invading the edges of curbs.
From my bedroom window
the bridge was a rigid iron arm
holding the bay in place.

The lower floor of my house
was a weaver's shop.
Girls would throw off their blouses
and spins threads on the grass.
The day I left,
one had her head blown away
by a sawed off shot gun
in a nine dollar robbery.

Objectives

But you seem concerned by specifics.
I have a car, yes,
and yellow sofas and chairs,
tables and tapestry rugs.

At noon the sun yawns lazy,
a soft layer of design
across walls and the flat
dull backs of my plants.

No, it's my own pen.
These? Pebbles I found
in the high desert where
the virgin rocks sleep,
near Barstow, on an abandoned
air field last week.
Just driving.

I could fit all that matters
into one bag.

Soon

I will be still soon.
I am ready as burnt red leaves,
edges arched like claws at the sky.
I will drift and fall
where there are no parking tickets,
divorces, infidelity or lies.
No fainting in public places
waking to nurses in pink sweaters
with wheelchairs and ammonia.

I want the dirt weight.
Land masses slide together.
The ice sheets shift.
New maps are printed.
But the cycle is old
and certain of itself.
The fine brown hand
of the earth covers.

There is no coughing,
no vision of birds,
aluminum or parking structures.
The bones are pure
and last forever.
In time lost pieces are reunited.
First secretions from sheets
then triangular nails bitten
and flicked across a rug.
The hair grows luxuriant.
It takes centuries
for the body to be complete.

Then I will soften
cell by cell.
Without double yellow lines,
checkbooks or felonies.
I will know the dirt.
It will be my right to refuse
roots and rebirths.
I will be a large forgetful worm.
I will burrow and be still.

Tracks

(after reading Blaise Cendrars)

The train tunnels dry clutter
from Paris to Vienna
from Baltimore to Philadelphia
down Bedford Drive in Beverly Hills.
The day is gigantic and borderless.
My heart pumps insanely, painfully
providing the rhythm,
the many sharp wheels.
I reel into noon, careen
and bellow down thin tracks.

I sleep-walk as all travelers
shoved into day, startled and dirty
pacing a doctor's waiting room.
My father is taking cancer tests.
Two hours late.
Four hours late.
Radium, barium, cobalt
the flesh jewels hidden
in the same brick building
I came to at fourteen
for a pregnancy test.
The doctor had daughters my age.
She telephoned my father,
threatened mental hospitals for girls
doing abnormal things in cars.
I sway with the motion,
rattle around hard curves
my teeth clenched and grinding
like engine parts.
Butchers wear white and doctors,
keepers of the meat and fish stain,
the same scrubbing up.

The train winds around a ridge
and streams through a gully.
It never stops.
It's an express.
No one is driving.
It just keeps going.
Silence is smashed by the black
whistle shrill at some indifferent
station.
Moths cough in an arc of light.
Smoky magnetic ruins stare back.
The familiar scattered bits.
Monstrous stripped flowers
in their own riptide,
opened, beckoning half faces
drilled with neon
tumbling and falling apart.
Weeds thrash.
One dead white arm waves
lost in steam.

Caroline Murphy's six year old hand
at dusk stepping off a curb
and walking under a truck.
The driver felt a small bump.
That's what made him stop.

Rittenhouse Square is always day-white.
The grass, the stone benches and statues.
My father wears baggy pants.
I bend in the crook of his arm,
my feet resting against his belt.
I am nearly one.
Our house is gray stone and brick.
Five steps to a wooden door.
A low wire fence to the sidewalk
and the Murphy's across the street,
later, in April, 1956.
Their father is a drunk.
Tommy wants to be a priest.
He's fifteen.
Teresa, Elinor, Louise, Charles
and Caroline, the baby.
She wears a white dress with a veil
and goes to a different school.
She takes me to confession,
baptizes my ragdoll.
We want to be nuns,
black gowned princess promised
to God, with his glorious stained
glass eyes, his chimes.
Daddy sends me to bed without supper,
yells Don't let those Catholics kids
touch you, ever.

I am big in the soft snow,
bundled and scarfed in the center
of blizzard sheeted Gowen Avenue.
The roofs are white,
the whittled branches
and buried cars.

Even the tracks below the hill
are white.
I won't let Caroline hold my doll.
She says I stuck nails
in God's hands.
We are watching the four fifty one train
impossibly black in the snow,
nun black, briefcase leather black,
black as the felt around my father's
wide brimmed winter hat.

There was a wind in April 1956.
Not cold,
I wear a short cotton dress.
But the branches are bent.
My shirt pushes towards the tracks.
Trash is caught in the low wire fence.
My father has the first cancer then,
can't talk or swallow, coughs blood.
The backyard is numb grey,
never planted though beds were cut
and something large and purple
pushed up the first year.
My bedroom faced the train station.
I had thin yellow curtains.
Caroline Murphy was dead.
When wind pushed the curtains open
I watched men with rolled up newspapers
climb the hill to their houses,
uncertain of solid ground.

The train cuts a path
to the Pacific.
I witness the breathless rage
of sunset when the bridges were consumed,
the maps and borders.
The train runs in a tight circle
powered by atomic fuels
radium, barium, cobalt.
It can grind its clipped metal
wings forever
while I sit at a window seat

crisscrossing the childhood
I carry like stage props
in my trunk.
Fat oak leaves spilling a greasy
pronged shade.
The cool sense of birth
before the first snow.
Flowers pulled from a priest's yard
who chased me half way home
in an August of fire flies
dying in jam jars.
The run over girl.
The stain in the street.
My six year old heart already shut.
I never cried,
even though she crossed the street
to visit me.
I'm rumbling down thin black metal grooves,
fine rows of black stitches weaving
through the contagion of my adolescence.
Over and over past
the hosed down stain
of Caroline Murphy.

I'm waiting for the white coated
conductor, for angels.
I'm waiting for the door to open
and my crippled womanhood
to at last push a smooth cheek
through the dry dirt.

VIRGINIA GILBERT

If I talk about my life as a poet and as an artist, what immediately comes to mind are the extreme joys and frustrations which such work involves. As a young person, I had always had a desire to create something of my own. Much of this stemmed from, first of all, a deep sense of history which I possessed. I grew up along a river in the midwest named after the Fox Indians. One of my older brothers was quite interested in finding Indian artifacts in the fields nearby. In our own yard, he and I both attempted to dig out the fragile remains of an arrowhead from beneath the bark of a tree only to watch it crumble at the edge of the knifeblade. Beside the back road leading down to our house sat an old wagon with "Riverside Drive" written in faded letters beneath the front seat. In the woods behind it, I found a board that came from a box, "U.S. Cavalry" labelled clearly on it. For me, these were all indications that something interesting and exciting had gone on before my time and I, somehow, wanted to recreate these scenes as well as become a part of them.

Then, too, I remember the unbusy summer weekdays when the river was not crowded with boats from Chicago, when the river was calm. I remember the nights, the full moon's face broken over the water, a train whistle echoing down river, the sudden, merciless storms and the trees bent over with the weight of wind and rain. These images became a part of me so it is no wonder that my first attempt at writing poetry took place, alone, in our family's rowboat out in the middle of the river which I loved. But it was not, however, until several years later, once again over water, being hit with a "sublime experience," that I finally found "the words," so to speak, and the encouragement to work seriously on poetry. There is such pleasure in finding beauty, in noting it, and, in turn, capturing it in a form of one's own making. Since then, my life has centered around poetry; I can never regret the excitement which comes to me, even today, from writing.

Of course, there are problems with being a writer. Technically, there are spells when nothing worthwhile gets put down on paper, when there is complete blankness. It is during such periods that the writer begins to have doubts of self worth and to wonder if the "magic" might not, indeed, be gone. Colleagues, as well, are not always the best of help. Ask any two people for their opinions on a new poem and one person will love line 3 for its tightness and the other will hate it for its flatness. Editors and rejection slips play notorious havoc with the egos of serious writers. I often think of F. Scott Fitzgerald in his New York apartment back around the 20's, pasting rejection slips (over 120) on his walls until he finally got his first story accepted for publication.

In another sense, too, the literary world can be awfully cold and impersonal until one has "made it" and stories abound about how unknowns have run elevators, worked as secretaries, driven cabs, and drivelled out language for ad agencies in order to support themselves while trying to become writers independent of such means of making a living. The contemporary way for a writer to earn some money is to land a good college teaching position (a feat which, in itself, is getting harder and harder to do these days). Between faculty meetings, appointments with students, classes, grading papers, and lesson planning, the writer gets to devote the remainder of the time to what is deemed most valuable, writing. Sometimes the world appears corrupt; the "sleep with me and I'll publish anything" syndrome; weak, "I got the money your mag. needs, how 'bout printing this"; or foolish (rumor has it that when Tennessee Williams submitted his dissertation, *The Glass Menagerie,* his faculty committee rejected it). Talent is not always easily recognizable.

Somewhere between the idealism of youth with its feelings that a poet is someone who always strives for perfection in both art and life and the realism of adulthood where pettiness often abounds amidst the starkness of the necessity of surviving, a precious quality or warmth may become replaced with something harsher and more demeaning, pessimism and bitterness. But, this works the other way around as well. A fierce devotion to one's writing, a genuineness of purpose, and a strength of character can also develop from such times of trial. I give credit to the person who endures in spite of the worst situations for it is not always easy to continue under this type of pressure.

Yet, when a poem or a story or a novel has been completed, it is impossible to not feel that, somehow, one's spirit is lifted out of the temporal body into a higher sphere, into the realm where the words, themselves, exist on an elevated, emotional level. This is what Emily Dickinson referred to when she wrote:

> If I read a book and it makes my whole body so cold
> no fire can ever warm me, I know that it is poetry.
> If I feel physically as if the top of my head were
> taken off, I know that it is poetry.

Such depth there is in this feeling! It is what makes everything else worthwhile.

Two Poems:
In Commemoration Of A Friend's Happiness

(for Ellen)

I.

In a Chinese Hanyak
herb hospital, the sick
want acupuncture. Our doctor
is friendly, knows the proper
locations, understands
the importance of heat, a red lamp's
quickness & its opposite.
With ginko tree limb, deer bone,
cinnamon, and the stem of a lotus,
a cure is formed.
The body grows.

II.

Irresistible, the earth carries
the weight of another planet.
Acknowledgement of blood
is precious. Born slight
within our positions,
the head is the first to unfold.
The legs are an eventual explosion.

Outside The Kampongs, At The Market, Waiting

(to Mrs. B.)

The shopkeeper hands you
a key. It is to a box
of black lacquer, a storm
painted on it, a crane

long-necking down the mote
to the darkness where

the reeds are hollowing
into a distant sea.

Impressions At Dawn

Here is the wooden
dirt bridge. And here
is the old man, laconic,
his ox and his cart
crossing. There is the sky,
a small branch
in his vest pocket.

Awakening, In A Church

I awake in a church in Quebec.
A Dominican monk stands over me.
He is a small wing beside me;
he is asking my name. Here, brother,
grains of wood run into my hand.
Here, I look for the worn stone
beneath the casket. *Father, I do not
speak French.* He speaks a little English.
My name is Ginny Gilbert. He understands.
I hear the grind of workmen
on the street outside. There are birds,
too, in the footsteps left
in the walls, in the creaking
of the ceiling. I touch
the plate glass keeping me
from the scarlet cloth. Yet,
the father is generous. . .
he offers me a meal. When I refuse,
he brings me an apple from the sleeve
of his cowl. In the morning, I play
with children on the Plains
of Abraham, the old battleground.

The Drought

It was
the morning
before
it rained
and Sam Smith,

farmer,
expected nothing
from the clumps
of clay.
And Sam

Smith, farmer,
walked
his fields
for the umpteenth
time, for

the seventh's
year worth
of dryness
he felt
flaking

from his skin
like pieces
of bark
flaking
from the dead

cottonwood,
his mother's
tree. And Sam
Smith, farmer,
knew

the precise
smell
of cattle
rotting, locust
like, by

the stock tanks,
near the caved-
in wells,
the long
forgotten streams.

And where
the earth
smelled
of heat, Sam
Smith knew

the suffering
of a sun
set
too high,
knew

the dust-
filled streets.
And Sam Smith,
a farmer,
searched

for a sign --
a stubborn
hawk rising
out
of the sullen

sky.

The Ritual

We can't be sure what
their meaning was, but we
can be sure they had meaning.

At the beginning, before I was nothing,
the great sky swelled my happiness.

Most figures are composed
of a single line that never
crosses itself, perhaps
the path of a ritual maze.

For this reason I left my hut
outside the barrios in the pre-dawn
of my existence, the new moon white
upon its shoulders.

> If so, when the Nazcas walked
> the line, they could have felt
> they were absorbing the essence
> of whatever the drawing symbolized.

In this distant ghostly light
I went to the fields to note
my life, the marks upon the sand.

> For according to their ways
> of thinking, a man's life-force,
> or soul, resided in his head.

So cracking two skulls together,
I prayed for fertility, the freedom
from boredom. My anthropomorphic hands
held no fat, it being the dry season.

> I shall bring you people
> without knees and they will
> defeat you.

They will defeat you, these gods
of the earth. The rain judges
our renewal.

Leaving, The Sepulchre City

The place was empty.
We entered the room
where the heads lay
upon the table,
formaldehyde, wrinkled.
The door closed behind us.

1.

What happened when the lieutenant
came over to you?

He asked me why
I hadn't killed the people yet.
I said, 'Sir, I didn't know
we were supposed to.'

What happened then?

Well, the lieutenant pulled
his automatic to his shoulder
and started shooting.

What did you do?

I started shooting, too.

How did you feel about shooting
all those people?

You get kind of used to it, sir,
used to the killing, that is.

But some of the men say you
were crying as you fired. Were you?

I don't know.
A lot of things were going on
around me -- a lot of people

running around and a lot
of noise all over the village.
I don't remember crying.

But you do remember
the people you shot, don't you?

Yes sir.

Would you say
most of those you shot
were adult men?

Some were.

Then the others were women
and children.

Yes.

How old were the children.

All ages, sir. Some
were, maybe, ten, eleven.
Some were in the arms
of their mothers.

Did you shoot them too?

Yes I did.

Did you think
that the children
were going to harm you?

No sir. But they
might have had a grenade planted
on them. You really
can't trust anyone, sir,
not anyone.

We have placed the people
in the corner, we have gone
around the bush to the other
steeple hidden by rocks and danced
upon the cave. We took off
our shirts and we took off our pants
and sat them by our feet. The brook
ran through the fire
but we knew it was good
and laid down with the girls.
We had no desire.

2.

Deep, in the earth,
it was broken
and we were men
painting buffaloes
on the slate rivers.

The women and children
slept near the fires.
The one behind me,
the one who walks
in the valley
beneath the shadow
of the big, yellow fire,
wraps our people
in dried skins.
We do not like
the air we cannot see
for it eats our people.
We do not like our blood
that shakes our bodies
over the animals
on the stones
for the elephant
chases us when he is hidden
and the small deer
who feeds us no longer
drinks from our lands.
We are empty
with bark, root, and berry.

3.

How many hours
is it? In the darkened hole
of the tavern, the men
sat on stools or stood
by the bar. The Budweiser
horses revolved around a table,
neighed once or twice,
then dragged their old cart
back home to the stable.
The women's band, just
finishing the last round
of drink was standing
by the wall, wailing
to the one, asleep,
laid, her back half bent
across the floor. The two men,
the two men close
to the window, kissed
each other's ear. The one
with two fingers opened
the other's graying shirt
and felt his breast, then,
seeing us outside staring in,
sensed the fear of the rising
wind, the last slow circuit
of the clicking of tin,
the last clicking of tin.

> *We were riding*
> *in the city then, along*
> *the lake, just before*
> *sunset. By the beach,*
> *we dug into the sands*
> *with our bones way*
> *past midnight.*

I came from the old buildings,
she said, and remembered them
along the drive. They are not
the same, no they are not, he said.
Now the city condemns them,

even drops the people's furniture
from the twelfth floor,
she said. They did that to me
without one thought for my dress
nor how well I could speak,
she said. Yes, I suspect
it is true, he said. People are
so cruel these days, so cruel.
The kids, they junk the new cars
along the streets, she said,
and throw rocks at your windows.
It is a shame it has come
to this, she said.
I have no home now, he said,
not since the war.
My parents think
I am dead, he said, yes, dead
because I deserted. That
can't be true, she said. No
it isn't but I love you.
Do you believe that, he said.
Yes I do. Will you let me,
he said. Yes, I want it.
Do you want me now,
he said. Yes, now, I need
you now, she said.

What happened when
you entered the car?

We talked about the weather.
It had been sleeting all day.

Did he touch you?

Yes, you could say that.

Where?

On the leg. He reached
over as though he
were fixing the tape deck
and bumped my knee.

What did you do then?

I tried to ignore him.

Did you?

Not really, I mean, he did it
again, this time more frantic
than before, putting his hand
on my calf and then, quickly
working it up a little
past the knee.

Did you like it?

What? I'm not sure
what you mean.

You understand what I mean.

Well, I was a little
scared. My stop was soon
and, when I went to get out,
he tried it again.

What happened then?

I got out.
I was pretty shook, then,
and just wanted to get away.
Even so, maybe out of habit,
I said, 'thank you'.

4.

She has tight,
protruding eyes. She is behind
the counter, holding
the ketchup bottle
near her hand. When we leave,
she follows us to the theater
where she plays a waitress

going out and going out
with a tray over her head.
You call out to her
but she is speaking
to her grandchildren,
at 29, the only performer
left alive.

(Untitled)

Somewhere
under my sleep
I am awake,
no longer the big
boned lady rattling
in the wind.

Somewhere
I have touched the water
running under me,
like a reed
floating downstream.

On my back,
I have known the sun
and have carried it
with me
past the cedars
and old pines.

SUSAN NORTH

Staying alive is the first thing. Really alive. All the doors open and no screens on the windows. Taking chances. Risking. Leaping. Finding out what is important for me. Discovering what I need.

You start out being someone's "child," a "sister," "student," "friend," "wife," "mother".....and one day you wake up and your label is lost in the sheets and you are swimming around inside a stranger. Fur grows on your palms, your feet sharpen into hooves, your scales glisten in the morning light. Maybe you can pull the covers over your head and this will be a bad dream. Maybe you can talk yourself into going on with whatever it is you're supposed to be doing and feeling.....but then your life never happens. You never happen.

I wanted to *be*. I had cut myself away from everything familiar and deadly. The debridement.....some of it bloody, violent, dangerous.....some of it drudgery, the minute disciplines, the cleaning of cupboards until under the labels and measurements, something else began to emerge, something that was *me*, solid as potato, textured and varied as asparagus. Then the possibilities bloomed. I began to make choices for myself.

I live in the desert and not by accident. I need space, silence, solitude. Mostly, I need mountains. But desert mountains -- with jackrabbits, spiny ocotillo, the relentless heat, the storms. When everything else falls out of my hands, the mountains remain.....and I climb into them at odd hours. A walk is a prayer. A coyote follows at his own distance.

The importance of distance, of solitude. A place to be, space for breathing. The spaces between the words. Making space, making each day. Making the minutes when I have to. Making possibilities where none exist. Allowing imagination, especially *emotional* imagination. Accepting long periods chalked up to endurance. Celebrating the small explosions of joy that pepper the days: the cat curled in my lap, the dry weeds by the road, lemonade, water running from the hose.....

Thankful for breath. Being alive is always a gift, a tenuous, mysterious gift. Reverence for the inexplicable.

The poems. Along with riding my horse in the desert, cleaning closets, caring for a few people very much, the poems are one of the ways I survive. They are involuntary, spontaneous -- usually happen very fast, often inconvenient, unexpected, contain surprises. I always believe each one is the last one. And always am thankful when it is not. The poems are explorations of places I cannot go in other ways. They keep things moving, give me a place to touch down, sometimes just plain get me through the night.

Hardest of all is trusting myself. Most difficult and absolutely essential. Slowly learning to say *yes*, learning to break the old habits of fear, the long time romance with despair. Learning to move with the momentum, trusting my instincts, my heart, my survival skills. Blessed with a passion for long shots and games of chance. Alive. Me. Lucky.

There Is A Point

when it is over

your vital signs cease
and what still moves is unimportant
somewhere in the debris of the closet floor
or failing to answer a letter
you have missed your last chance

you don't remember the circumstance
but you know now there is
nothing you can have
that you want

no one is concerned
your motions convince them everything is the same
you go through Christmas in the new car
Friday nights with the Millers
then it is summer and you drive children
back and forth to the beach

one evening you stay too long in the shower
dinner boils over and changes nothing
that night you leave you have been gone a long time
and will not return

It Isn't That You Don't Understand

the doctor has explained
and your sister has been
more than patient
your husband carries you
like a porcelain bowl
his cheeks stuffed
with vouchers of devotion
everyone is cheering
you can do it

and you could
on the doctor's couch
or riding in the boat of your husband's arms
you wanted to be the one who grew back
and recovered with time
but the rug lifts like a magic carpet
and all your beans spill
your clothes collapse on your bones
your breasts empty their sacks

you remember these warnings
but it is the phone or the pills
you grit your teeth and hold up
your end of the conversation
but it's over
someone turns out the light
and you shine in the dark

the arguments hold water
and you go under
holding your breath you dive
to the other side of the lake
they wave handkerchiefs and persuasion
but you are dreaming now
the dark flags of water under your oars

when you never wake up
they will know there was more to it

The Truth Of The Matter In Coolidge, Arizona

Her neighbors are telling the truth:
she is filthy,
stinks, garbles her words
and can barely find her way home.

The "tin can lady" crawls
inside garbage cans, goes down
the alleys on her hands and knees.
The children giggle and the braver
throw stones at her old yellow dog.

By Friday she has enough rags and cans
for bus fare to the prison. Every week
she comes to see him, every week
telling the guards:
my boy a good boy is innocent.

And he is.

When Your Husband Goes To Prison

your friends are sympathetic
solicitous at first
each one has *a friend you would like*
they keep reminding you
nine years is a long time and no one would expect

your mother gives advice
where he went wrong and why
you can only save your skin
by answering yes yes yes yes

triumphantly she asks
how can you live this way
as though there is another

your life becomes the letter
you write and do not mail
what cannot be said
grows in the envelopes
soon it walks the edge
of every bitter visit

you no longer remember the beginning
or what part you are playing

one night you dream
there is a giant conspiracy
his brother, his son, the lawyer in his black suit
the other woman gives testimony
you turn state's evidence
dragged in on oath you answer
every question they will not ask
an agreement is reached

they will trade
his body for yours

your mouth closes its envelope
the letters wrap you in wet sheets
thrashing in the darkness you call
for your friends for your mother

and they come

After Ten Years

Your mother flies from Boston to Phoenix.
This is her only trip to the prison.

She says: *You look fine. They must be treating you well.*
She is asking: *Can you live through this?*

You tell her: *Things are not too bad.*
She translates this accurately: *I am doing whatever I can to survive.*

You tell her the food is good
and Saturday morning you play tennis.
She talks about the Jazz Festival and how
the cars still go right past the house all day long.

Neither of you mention
the stabbing last week
or how old she looks.

Near the end of the visit
she cannot hold back any longer:
You broke your father's heart.

When she goes through the steel door,
she waves.
You will not see her again.

For Michael

you write again
I fold your letter into my pocket
and lean against the warm shoulder of my horse

there is rain
and fifteen years of silence
stumbling through a foreign country
making gestures
always paying too much unable to bargain

suddenly you are the one from home
speaking the language I remember
I can tell you everything

somewhere in these pages my heart
has been pressed it is a moth

when my hands darken and tremble
they call the names of drowned sailors
of men sodden and abandoned in bars

all the women in my family drink
and wave melodic Irish names like warnings
they have tiny waists and long slender thighs

how did I come
sober and thick among them
Kathleen, Molly, Mary Lynn

it is your stance
your shoulder turned into the wind
and it is
the wind

with one *gently* you engage my violent private heart

I have begun to practice small deprivations
tea without sugar half as much sleep
days of deliberate hunger

when you need these skills
I will be absolutely dependable

Farmers' Almanac, Or A Guide To Loving

do it carefully
when you choose
the fiction to feed your life
keep in mind   *resistance to drought*
susceptibility to disease
above all check this label
   can withstand
   long periods of neglect

prepare the earth
memorize the predictions
of waxing and waning

do not expect anything
what the rain brings to others
may never be yours

for lightning observe the standard precautions
   when your hair stands on end
   fall to your knees
   you may pray but touch nothing metal

when you come to the friable days
rebuild your fences rekindle the rust
never invest more
than you can afford to lose

Aunt Lenore At Forty-Five

I don't know where I found the nerve.
At the end of aisle eleven,
shoestrings and toothpaste in one hand,
I reached for the package of condoms.
Driving home, I heard whispers.

The blinds were drawn,
the foil tore easily.
It looked so harmless,
almost delicate.

I don't know what to do with the others.
It is wasteful to throw them away,
but I don't know anyone
to give them to. How did I miss
what there is so much of.

Still, I thought I should know what they looked like.

Small Poem For Michael

shadows deepen the road like water
there are hours between us
but your face stays with my hand

charcoal on vellum no. 2
the sinew of the blue heron
the last clear water held in a hoofprint

you are perfectly grey feather
caught on the ledge of the thirtieth floor
and the wind that takes it

the hours of light prepare in the mountains

Poem For Her Thirty-Fifth Birthday

1.

the song starts when you know
how to hold one note
and believe you will need
nothing else

but you complain you have walked
the night with a stone in your shoe
thinking hunger would lead you

you are counting your ribs again
never the same number
your choices are closer together
each year they are thinner

you suspect they dye their hair
but you cannot be sure
you have nothing else to go on

2.

you return to your poems
bearing gifts asking permission
to open one more
you hurry there are poems hiding in hubcaps
in the shoes at the back of your closet
poems balanced on the rim of your glass
you must find them they will not last forever
you feel a poem growing painfully under your toenail

tonight you will write it
will dedicate it to the stone in your shoe
to the woman who wants to but won't
you will dedicate it to all the heroes in your life
they have always been men
but are never the ones you sleep with
you dedicate it to your numberless ribs
that have no straight answers

Ascent

> "There is always
>   the possibility of joy. . ."
>   Michael Hogan

when it begins it will be
a foreign language of careful conjugations
your comprehension will exceed your vocabulary

the dictionary is your map
slowly and deliberately teach yourself
the words for *joy* for *lemon*
for *salmon laughter silk*

love each one shamelessly
unwrap each possibility
this is a birthday
these are presents
new and awkward on your tongue
they grow rich and sweet with use

push for joy be relentless
be ruthless when you must
leave friends sworn to grief
go alone if necessary
insist on *sky*
push for joy plant it everywhere
sing it bounce it spill it into each cupped hand

lose your fear of saying *I am happy*

RACHEL MAINES

    Tyer-in and *Textile Women* are the two thematic poems of my work, the most closely identified with my obsession with textiles and women's history.

    The tyer-in or web drawer in a textile mill is largely an ex-occupation due to increasing mechanization, but those few drawers-in that remain are nearly all women. The tyer-in threads in thousands of warp yarns on the loom prior to weaving; she pulls each yarn end through a tiny heddle eye with a hook according to a particular pattern called a "sett", pulls it through a grate called a reed, and ties it to the cloth beam on the front of the loom. The task requires tremendous concentration and is vital to the operation of a weave shop. If even one thread is out of place, hundreds of yards of fabric may be ruined, and neither the tyer-in nor the weaver will receive full pay for the day's work, as both are paid by the piece, on "incentive". Drawing-in is typical of the kind of highly-skilled, low-paid, tedious, isolating, detailed, one-pointed tasks that form the greater part of the labor by which women support society.

    Textile Women expands on this theme by relating the imprisonment of women in alienating, undervalued jobs to their sexual and economic captivity in marriage. The half-title honors the almost superhuman courage of women organizing against the textile patriarchy, trade union women whose victories and defeats move me powerfully.

Textiles are an archetype of women's labor: they are a taproot through which the male economic and social hierarchy draws strength and nourishment from the creative energies and productivity of women. They are one of the most essential elements of the human environment, intimate shelter, the medium of comfort and protection from nature's assault on the body. Women's historical interaction with them is potentially explosive and terrifying to male culture; there is too much magic and mystical knowledge in the textile relationship. My own passion for the textile is all-consuming and my gratitude to its creators beyond expression. My work as a textile historian and administrator of a textile study center is a celebration of this relationship, and these two poems represent a kind of passionate overflow of feeling from profession to poetry, poetry that professes textiles.

As a textile historian, my efforts are aimed at making women aware of their value as artists, workers and creators of culture, reaching them through the medium so long associated with the home and with "women's work." Needlework and textiles have much in common with poetry: the crafting of fine detail, the half-hidden meanings and images, the radicalism couched in symbols only women understood, concealed and camouflaged for the critical male eye. The needlewoman dares to turn male imagery upon itself, she dares to be beautiful and to be funny. Much of my poetry attempts to parallel the insouciance of needlework, especially in the humorous work such as *Finders Keepers* and *Schrafft's.*

Tyer-in, Textile Women, and *Union Educator* developed out of a long association with a textile union and show clearly my fascination with technical and specialized vocabularies. I find the concreteness of technical language very satisfying, especially to express emotional abstractions. All of this group of poems, except *Schrafft's* and *Almost Newyork,* contain words with double meanings where the ambiguity is intentional. Sometimes this duality has a humorous purpose, as in the "rites of labor" or the luggage which is "terminally lost," but often the words will represent an intersection of more than one serious meaning. My early studies in Latin and Greek left me with a continuing interest in the psychology of language and a conviction that whenever a language uses one word to mean two or more things, it is because those things are somehow seen as the same. The most common duality of meaning in my recent work is the word "union," which refers not only to a labor organization, but to all forms of social and personal union including sexual union.

Almost Newyork is the only poem in this group written before November, 1974, when all hell broke loose.

Not at all coincidentally, my mother is Natalie L. M. Petesch, the now well-known feminist fiction writer. She taught me (a) independence (b) grammar and spelling (c) respect for women and (d) how to send manuscripts so that the post office doesn't bend them, among other things too numerous to mention.

Textile Women:
(Lowell, Lawrence, Fall River, Amoskeag, Gastonia, Marion,
Columbia, Oneita)

      did you ever wonder at the woolen flannels
at the archetypical elegance of noils
      at taffetas,
   yarn-dyed and striped
   restless and harsh against the light?

         in the passion of lives,
            did your distaff hands find again
            the sheets
        woven in agony
           the blankets
             thrown to the floor
      the draperies and hangings
            of your marriage bed?

      you have survived me
         between us the yarn
         is all unwound
stretched crosswise through
      time there is great
               comfort
    in the damasks
      and brocade
    you have created from the filaments

    of unthinkable darkness

almost newyork

almost newyork with sagging arms
   old women from our windows
      full of washing

      we talk

moishe is in the yeshiva today
      giovanni
      giovanni
        your mamma's calling
     we died
   before the ghetto became white america

our geraniums bloom
   soot-spotted where we
reel the long
   white lines alley to alley
  scream momentarily
   and next day smile
   to see you
   to see your children
   your ghetto eyes

Schrafft's, Third Avenue and East 57th Street

a place of women and toast
husbands divorced and divorcing
fruit salad on transparent plates

the butter spreads like mercury
eating alone at these tiny tables is
like dancing without a partner
a game of poker played like solitaire

the men leave quickly after lunch
even executives know their place
and everyone here knows better than to say
that talk is cheap

the union educator

the magician of labor, you arrive
   in a shower of pamphlets and
            folding chairs
   in this union,
      an act of tenderness
      you perform to a calliope
            of slamming shuttles and
           roaring cards

    in the margins of contracts you
         explain
         the brotherhood of history
         the binding weft of sorrow

the rites of labor fill this hall like
   fly in a weave shop
   you stand among the looms
   a robed priest projecting
     songs against the ceiling and interpreting
      for us the meaning
      of this passionate communion

Finders Keepers

woolen and secure
you are walking in Brooklyn
starting your maroon car,
catching planes and cursing savagely
as your baggage is terminally lost.

I think it is here, the suitcase you
cannot find, a tweed
browner than your eyes. Its steel locks
attract me; I sit reading the tags --
Bemis, Tennessee. Cincinnati, Ohio.
Kannapolis and Raleigh, the handwriting
of clerks and baggage handlers
you do not remember.

Surely you would not know if I opened it,
you would blame the disarray
on careless porters, if I unfold your
shirts of cotton damask and Oxford cloth,
plug in your razor and watch the blades spin,
lay your t-shirts reverently
across the table, examining their
folds and neckbands, every one dignified
with a union label,

marvelling at the smallness of your socks.

Meanwhile, you are pacing the terminal
in Georgia, inventing profanity,
restless in the spring
weather, stalking up and down in
the same suit as yesterday,
making it moist and fragrant,
the fabric of rage, to which
I could never be near enough.

RSVP

for your Easter vacation, I would like
to invite you to Tahiti for a week of
mangoes and sunshine, splashing the Pacific
in each other's faces, making love before
dinner with the terrace door open, the
curtains rustling in the prevailing westerlies.

to get there, I will blackmail a
ship's captain, an upright Yankee with
a shameful past, to stow us away in
a luxury cabin. For the duration, we
will walk the decks with great dignity,
arm in arm, discussing the difference
between the porpoise and the dolphin.
At midnight, we will be sitting astern,
hidden behind a lifeboat, French kissing like
teenagers in the back seat of a Chevy.

on the way to the dock in San Francisco,
I will rent a tandem bicycle, to
get us over the Great Plains and the
Rockies; you will wear blue jeans and
a loose shirt. The sun will darken your
freckles and in the moonlight I will
trace the edges of your sunburn with my teeth.
Pedaling along behind you, I reach under
your shirttail for the curve of your
back, and your steering wobbles.

Mark your calendar and return the
engraved card at once; there are reservations
and connections to make and I
must know right away whether I can expect
the pleasure of your company.

2-15-43/2-15-76

there must have been a battle somewhere
in France or the Pacific; soldiers
took time out from pillage and rape
to send valentines to mothers and sweethearts.
Women shovelled their walks and watched
as Western Union rang the bell next door.
While we all edged over the Piscean cusp
Jimmy Hoffa was blowing out candles.
Later, some irate candle would return the favor.

The hospital was concerned about the unusual birthmark.
Very few babies have union labels at birth,
fewer still sit up and argue with delivery-room nurses.
Your mother did not smile as she recalled
heavy nights in June and buying her fall wardrobe
in the maternity department. Your father,
mischievously proud of having fostered a Y chromosome
at the appropriate moment,
leers at the receptionist and brings flowers.

This year, the ground hogs await your coming.
The Aeneid is rewritten as a labor romance,
merchants hang hearts on their sleeves and
in their windows a day late,
the postal service takes another Monday holiday,
and somewhere in Italy they are trying to
decide how to spell your name in a language
no one remembers.

the tyer-in

the music of the drawing-in
she knows the loops and eyes
    the shuttle and sheds
the dangerous passage across the warp

the days lengthen out like roving across the room
        shafts of sunlight thicken with fly
she remembers hours
    of silence when no one sang
    except the loom

DONA STEIN

The poems I have here are about loss -- by death, age, pickling, by transformation, by argument, discovery, sleep, and by grief. I think they are also about gain by the same methods. Reading again other poems of mine not here, I see them as about the threat of violence and disorder present, destruction from without and within, the longing for security in love, and the immobility of helplessness. Now and then, the poems express delight, joy. I'd like to go into detail about some of the poems that follow.

For F.J.L. describes my father's death and the grief and sadness that separation can never change. Also presented is a mythic fear: the beloved dead is not really dead, just asleep. Because he lives on unaged in my heart, my father still drives a car, still laughs -- all dream surprises and sometimes waking ones. I wonder if other people visit cemetaries "to make sure"; yes, the wake, the funeral were real. How we magically hope against that knowledge!

The wish to preserve people and situations is in *Putting Mother By* also. I had fun writing this poem after I discovered how simple it is to make half-sour pickles. Of course, I remembered fairy-tale stereotypes. My brothers and sisters are presented as dwarves, our mother as an all-knowing giantess.

Night Garden With Ladies is based on a dream I had

after a family gathering with many aunts, uncles, cousins, nieces and nephews. Some of the description of sweaters, aprons, and tools is directly from the dream, but based, I am sure, on the memory of a grandmother's attire and her difficulty as a large woman standing up again after kneeling in the earth for some time. In the dream were pieces of conversation from the family gathering -- not put directly into the poem. When I was young, these people were seen by me as powerful; most of the women in my family were strong and had to be. Often they were raising children alone. In the dream, they emerged as fury-like figures: people I did not want to appease by a conventional life, despite feeling their disapproval. The dream ended abruptly. The poem's ending was a problem. I worked on it for almost a year, off and on. How was I going to get these women out of my poem? For the dream, I woke up. So I knew the ending for the poem -- I had light arrive. It seemed the only possible solution.

Carol's House is a description of my sense of space in a barn house. Carol lives in a barn with 50' heights for some living areas, with catwalks and gangways connecting the other living areas where haylofts used to be. The barn is surrounded by trees and fields. Within, people are surrounded by trees in tubs and by space and light. Parts of the barn rose like a ship when I looked back from a lower field. These perceptions came together with some literal facts of direction, fence and sunflowers.

An example of a simple image causing a lot of work is *van Gogh Painting.....* I pictured van Gogh painting a river across a room. The river becomes real, an avenue for escape. I liked the image and the connotations of water purifying and healing. Then I spent weeks reading about van Gogh's work, examing the few originals I could and the reproductions. I re-read van Gogh's letters. He was at times permitted the freedom to go to the fields to paint, so there was no need for him to escape confinement. When I read that, I thought I should abandon the poem because fact did not support fancy. Then I realized it did not matter and I would write the poem anyway. The poem is also about illness and suffering, and supposes art can alleviate both. The poem used the notion of room as a womb and ends with re-birth.

In the Year of the Tiger is obviously a sestina. It was an exercise I struggled with for some time until I realized I had been proceeding the wrong way. I had started with the end words instead of with the story I had wanted to tell. When I abandoned concern for form and concentrated on what I wanted to say, the poem was written with some minor changes and deletions. For a form that has always been difficult for me, this poem seemed to work and seemed to have come about fairly effortlessly, once I knew my mistake.

Working in forms is challenging. Each time I've tried a new form, I've learned something more about the uses of language: what one word in a certain place can do, how the pauses of contemporary speech can be used. And when to forget being restricted by the form. My new manuscript (*Children of the Mafiosi, West End Press*) includes another sestina, a villanelle, and a madsong. I have yet to write either an Italian or Shakespearean sonnet I care for. Those challenges still await.

Night Garden, With Ladies

They are busy in the moon
whispering, laughing

digging around the tulips,
the roses. They have round

faces, heavy bodies; they
wear cotton stockings

and take a long time standing
up again. Their tools lean

in apron pockets; heavy sweaters
on in the cool air, their faces

streaked from work in the night
earth, I know them well,

their dark competence. They
are my aunts, my three grandmothers,

and their talk with each turn
of the trowel is of the cousins,

our fates. They are relentless,
yet say they want success,

happiness. They treat all the roots
alike, and when the sky

becomes light green and the trees
lift themselves from blackness,

they move off into the air,
their arms up, hair flying after.

Lady And The Wolf

I am in my lady skin coming
Down my ordinary stair,
My thigh level, perpendicular

To the wall. At the door
You are in your wolfskin,
Your red eyes glow, your pelt

Bristles above your tie, and
Your ears are luminous
From the moonlight; coming

Down the hall I hear a hum,
A singing motion of silk,
Of fur. Prancing behind

Me in your bark and blood
Colored tie, you pant toward
My neck and before we reach

A proper door, I hear a tooth
Sharp zip and see my lady
Skin on the floor. You unbutton

Your wolfskin, hasty paws
Fumbling, and we stand staring
At what pure forms our souls are in.

van Gogh Painting His Way Out of the Asylum

First, he paints the concrete
floor brown. Then with grey
he puts on stones, sticks,
and with purple, their shadows.

Next, he works on one wall. He
places outlines of trees, but
forgets it is spring and has their

bare branches scrape the ceiling.
It is both day and night on the ceiling.
In the middle, he puts the warm

ruff of the sun, then half the sky
is black with colored planets
blinking off and on. He saves

escape for last; it is a river
starting like a stream with
watercress in the right-hand corner

of the cell; it grows wider
and deeper as it crosses
the floor. He lays down his paints,

takes off his trousers. The water
is full of sun as it rises
up the wall; van Gogh laughs

as he puts one foot into
midnight, the other into morning.
Splashing, he pushes one wall

behind. He turns on his back
kicking his way out of the room;
carrying within what cruises

like the shadow of a great
destroyer, he leaves everything
behind, moving on the river
that leads to the sea.

Visiting M. At The Happy Valley Nursing Home

That pink curtain, she says,
Reminds her that when she
Was middle-aged she used

To dream she was dancing
In a costume; waiting

In the wings, she could
Feel the heat from the audience
Then gliding to center stage,

Effortlessly and flawlessly
She performed the routines

She learned at Miss Bootsie
MacDonald's School of Tap
and Toe in Jefferson Missouri

At the turn of the century;
There was wild applause:
She saw her brother Harry

With his hands before his face
And her mother's face, a shining
Blur; she says she would wake

Up as she skipped to the wings
Still hearing applause in the blue

Bedroom in Flint, Michigan,
And wanted to wake the snoring
Shape beside her; why wasn't

He clapping too? She says she
Felt so light and happy
She would go back to sleep
Until the factory whistle blew.

Putting Mother By

We are in her kitchen;
we have one enormous
pot and all the spices
are together.

We are too tiny and take
so long to sterilize
the jar; finally, more

water is boiling, waiting.
We don't have to call,
she hears and comes
into her kitchen.

We lift her over the pot;
she slips into the water
without a murmur.
She does not try to get out.

Later, we stand on tiptoes
and watch her inside
the Mason jar floating
in liquid by bay leaves
and flakes of pepper.
Dill weed floats like
a pine tree around her hair.

We look at each other, we
press our noses against
the jar and see she is more
surprised than anything else.

Carefully we carry her down
into the cellar; we store
her next to the peaches and plums:
we have her now.

For F.J.L.
(May 7, 1919 - May 2, 1972)

Your heart faltered, attacking
itself, you, a victim of your
own muscle; you became slow
motion, sighed, turned toward a sofa
and lay down. That was it.

I was afraid you still heard
your own pulse in your ear,
could feel the ridged brocade,
still saw the ceiling, and wondered
about what was beyond the roof.

I would have knocked on your coffin
like a door whispering, "wake up,
Father, wake up. Can't you tell
it is Spring and your birthday?"

In the Year of the Tiger

In the Year of the Tiger, we have our last fight
at the narrow table with blue
oilcloth, an ashtray between us,
the heavy November night pouring down outside.
"I'm leaving, this's it, I'm leaving,"
you shout, waiting for me to stop you.

Beyond despair, I want to laugh at you,
try not to giggle, "go ahead!" The chairs know this fight,
all the pauses. Upsetting one, leaving,
you stomp upstairs. I push the ashtray around swirls of blue
in the cloth, light a cigarette. Outside
wind moans, doing my crying for us.

Drawers are being yanked open, shoved closed. Us,
I try to think: me, you.
Rain like shot begins to pour outside
becoming sleet. Sheepish, you come down, fight
back incongruity: "Where's the brown suitcase, the blue
one, then?" You say, "I'm still leaving!"

Why is it taking him so long to pack, I wonder, leaving
the table, restless, half wanting to be done with us,
mindlessly wiping ashes off the blue
and white cloth. It's still. I imagine you
staring at the razors in the bathroom's procelain glare. I fight
pity, fear, giving in, and wait outside

myself listening to some ticking inside; outside
the steady pocking of sleet: upstairs, a helpless shuffle leaving.
I turn my back unwilling to watch your uncertain fight
with terror, with surprise: us,
finished; I'm letting you go, you!
And I am free at last; my hand moves on the blue

oilcloth like a bird practicing in blue
air. At last I hear your step outside
the kitchen door. I suspect you
have changed your mind and don't want to leave;
frightened, you can't imagine us
apart and need me; you fight

through watery blue eyes for some way to dignify not leaving,
mention the drumming rain outside, how it's been us
together for so long, how you (now crying) can't finish this fight.

Map
(for Matthew)

There is no place we can
look for you, not in the bones of your twin,
not in the smile of your little brother;
we cannot trace you in the shape
of your father's head or the color of
your mother's eyes; you will not
be on a road of your town bicycling
to meet a friend or on the pond
behind your house; you will row
across a little sleep dear child,
and when you bump the other shore
there will be others -- they will
show you places beyond grief
and everywhere you will hear
singing, Matthew, singing.

Carol's House

If you have been there,
you know the bed rises
each night according

to the moon and leaves
the bay due south.
It leaves the barking

dogs, the steady click
of the electric fence,
the ghostly slats

of the corn crib; it floats
past six heavy light
houses, the dead sunflowers.

It travels so far out to sea,
not even the most ardent
sailor can bring

the quilted deck back
before dawn, and when
we awaken, not even

you know what I have heard
and seen. If you have
been there, you know this

is possible, and that I
kneel on the deck toward the east
to tell this again and again.

ELIZABETH KEELER

Writing poems is like REM sleep. That is, apparently necessary for survival. Freud spoke of "the dream work" in regard to an aspect of the dreaming which comes with REM sleep, but this is work which cannot be scheduled and remains outside my sometimes cumbersome tables of organization and procedures for ordering the rest of my life. I never have any notion when I will be moved to start a new poem nor when a sense of certainty will come that I have "finished" one in progress. I only know both these phenomena will occur.

In contrast to other Writing -- which I coax myself to do by providing attractive corners of the house where light and sky will fall on the page, etc. -- I'm fairly indifferent to where I'll be when I put down those first lines of a poem; and the issue of judgment of the poetry -- good poem, bad poem -- also is somehow analogous to the Acts of God clauses on insurance contracts: people don't ordinarily sit around judging the Acts of God and whether He should have or shouldn't have but opt out of responsibility for these things and see what they can do in relation to these events, to the cataclysmic goings-on of Forces Outside Oneself.

I'm not clear at all on how I became a poet. I know -- partly recollection, partly Mother's anecdotes -- that at

age 3 or 4 I was already engaging her at bedtime by telling her new "pomes" and that my brother (who other-
wise seemed to have it made) was jealous. That had to be
marvellously gratifying. On the other hand there was a
price to be paid for my mother's attention. She used to
laugh as I got to the last lines, and I was very offended.
(Her excuse was that she would be feeling certain I
couldn't bring off the rhymes; yet I would. It cut no ice
with me then and possibly still doesn't.)

I took myself with high seriousness throughout my
childhood. Had no tolerance at all for listeners inclined
to laugh at the ending of my paean to Zeus (circa 3rd
grade, when our class in my progressive school studied
ancient Greek culture.) My ending lines were:

    with his long robes a-flowing
    while he his nose is blowing.

Now that I'm older, I have more sense of fun about
myself but poetry is still a serious enterprise for me. I
scorn the Open Reading, still prevalent in California, because -- well, partly because they are often boring and
often vicariously painful like Mark Twain's description in
Joan of Arc of a stranger coming uncertain of welcome
into a great house -- but really because there is an impli-
cation that the (sloppy) pot-inspired poem someone has
made up between one a.m. and dawn this morning,
spurred on by the opportunity to read it to real live
people today, is a marvellous poem. This strikes me as
similar to a persistent American belief that a child pro-
digy's production is somehow more successful and moving because it occurred precociously; that newness is
somehow greatness.

The rebuke to seriousness of a hasty effort offends me,
I guess. (At the same time I don't at all deny that some
poems, perhaps the most lyric and strongest ones, are
born full blown and scarcely in need of revision, soldiers
out of dragon's teeth. *That* seems to me a different phe-
nomenon.) I can't tell to what extent my disapproval of
the one to six a.m. production prior to the chance to
read gets connected with some persistent confusion I
have about the subject of Who Listens to poems, Who
Reads poems, and how important it is to me to be Heard,

and, even assuming I could settle these issues, which I can't, how much influence do people's reactions have on me.

In a documentary I often think about, Robert Lowell said to James Dickey that writing poetry is like caring for a garden -- it's for you, not others. That remark seemed wonderfully perceptive to me. But as a gardener, now and then, I would like people to see some particularly wonderful roses I have, or how a seedling redwood -- which chose me, my yard -- has grown 15 feet high in a few years. And I often puzzle about the question how much it means to me to have listeners, readers, a chance to speak through my poetry to people of my time. I've always known I would like that; that being with people in that way is attractive.

On the other hand being heard through my poetry has become less important to me since the spring of 1973 when I completed a long poem I didn't doubt was a good poem, a strong poem, and had this strange confidence re-inforced by the fact that three little magazines almost simultaneously decided to print it. After that confirmation that I was indeed a poet, I felt freed to concentrate on making my poems have as much evocative power and significant meaning to me as possible; creating what I felt were good, strong poems, with little regard for other people's hearing them or judging them.

This attitude was reinforced that fall when a return-address envelope arrived from *Loon Magazine*. It obviously contained a manuscript I'd sent out. I spotted it in the mail, experienced a fall in spirits, and was tempted not to open the envelope at all and thereby evade the ego blow rejection brings. I remember bitterly regretting not having stopped while I was ahead.

Of course I did open the envelope, and I found that *Loon* had accepted a group of my poems and were mere-ly returning the others. That was very pleasing, but I've continued to act along the lines of the keenly experienced recrimination that autumn day -- taking very few risks. I don't submit poems to editors unless invited.

Another aspect of my poetry both puzzling and inter-esting to me right now has to do with myself as a listener or reader. I find that I tend not to *remember* other people's poems, or at least their titles, irrespective of how much pleasure and excitement I may have experienced in reading or hearing them. I may not even remember the poet's name. Mark McCloskey wrote a poem, *This Year*, which I liked so much I typed it over and stored it in the cupboard where I keep copies of my poems and some of the work of friends which I truly value. Yet I only know the poet's name is Mark McCloskey and the title of the poem is *This Year* by virtue of going back to that cupboard and bringing out the page.

Then there's the poem *Seasonal* by Edward R. Weismuller, printed in either *Harper's* or *Atlantic Monthly* during World War II. It engaged me passionately, although I've never known why, and at the time I attempted to memorize it. At times during the next ten years some fragment of it would come back to me, usually the first lines but sometimes the last:

Puts on nostalgia like a dragging cloak
And thinks cold thoughts of death

During the 1950's, proceeding from my inexact recollection of the first lines but definite recollection of the subject matter, I set myself the task of locating the poem itself in *Reader's Guide to Periodical Literature*. The quest had the obsessive qualities, and the pleasures of discovery, of a treasure hunt.

The point of all this is that my forgetfulness about poets and poems obviously is not a matter of faithfulness per se. I have an idea the reason for it may be that poems come as dreams -- carrying a poignant valence to the dreamer at the time of the dreaming and often for several days. Then, as the dream's connections to a past time and a present time are fuzzed and blurred and weakened, the dreams fade away and are forgotten until redreamed of remembered when some aspect of current reality re-evokes a vital experience.

I find myself wanting to end this statement with some lines of *Phantoms* which engages itself in the mysterious equivalences between dream and persistent poignant images:

> The night dreams come as ivory gulls
> making their long cries and yielding nothing
> to present time. I am
> still married and the children are green
> water sprouts wild with growing,
> great delicate leaves on puny stems
> in my dreams, my gulls.

Those lines please me, as the whole poem does, and again the reasons for my gratitude are mysterious to me. This perception reinforces my sense that the most fulfillment in writing or reading poetry comes with the possibility of accepting the poet as him/herself -- a specific voice with a specific experience to convey. It is a point at which the need to be judgmental -- to decide whether the poem is good or bad; to think how the poem might have been much better -- falls away, leaving poet or listener with the rare and precious chance to be intimate with self or another for a moment of time.

LIGHT

In December I needed light.
Trapping it became the end of every afternoon.
I risked the mountain roads
which brokenly went towards sunlight.
I dodged the trees which drank it up
I climbed the rocks it seemed to lie beyond.
I poached on lands protected by wire and words and dogs.
Craft? I was craft. I was Indian.
If light had been a rabbit, running free
in fields, I'd swing it by the ears.
Quiet? I was silence. Gentle? I was milk
flowing to love the pursed greed of a child.
Light was not enticed. Its grains
dissolved to liquid draining
in the dirt before my feet. And earth
looked up at me with stony dusty face.
All I wanted was light. Lacking,
I met my shadow -- On the roads, in the woods,
on the rocks, in the fields.
My darkness looked at me.

Looking For Light
And Finding The Sea

1. Connecticut

Lucite clothespins color this September sky.
I must gather them like leaves and take them
to the new land.
Clothespins are my past, correctly summer
when it is summer and winter when blood runs thick.
I heard of a New England year when frost held through July.
Potatoes finally planted, withered and snow fell
in August.
If next summer comes, I will not be here waiting.
I am leaving this place where love, gray fox,
slipped over the field's stone wall into woods,
and the sea comes in and goes out.

Where what I have learned is useful --
civilized basements spring freshest in March; the Sound
is cold in May but keeps a warmth into October.
(The sea, gray substance, is more than friend.
Beautiful -- it drowns and is beyond touch
as my father was.) I am going away.
To States colored red and orangutan orange,
also yellow, on the map in my mind.
There is an ornate compass inscription on the horizon
of my map, and in it I am the force running rusty
but still expectant beneath the iron arrow.

Autumnal Claque

For nine days it rained
and this morning.
Then, came the crows!
Raucousness and black
almighty clapping of wings.
They take my walnut tree
and sing, sing about its produce.
Or perhaps the elevation.
Last year they chose persimmons.
As I watch, they fly away.
I can't imagine what
tomorrow's skies may bring
nor if the shocking pleasure
of praise will again offend me.
I take the bridal garland from my hair
and sort the wash.

Snow In Marin County!

For two nights it snowed
on our green local mountain.
Today the fireroads
flowered with children.
And I caught joy like measles.

I thought I was too old,
life too mortal,
me too serious.
Swollen and smiling,
I have a child's disease.

Again, Flowering

This great hunger for chocolate seizes me.
Huge silver foil slabs of it. I eat.
The marvellously flowering plum tree
pleasuring me through my bedroom window
takes place, I discover, on my side
of the barbwire fence. It is mine.
So I wear out my shoes in museums
of Oriental art, making myself accountable
to my son's father. Our lives teeter
on my finding a Chinese scroll where the path
into the mountains never plunges down.
Where blossoms preserve in Eastern inks
a different April than the spring we flawed.
(There were other waters in which we loved.)
In some dynasty with some brush stroke
a master hand must have drawn beginnings
which never give way to leaves and never
before October fall.

**The Mountain In My Head,
Its Periodic Loss**

With heavy instruments of mind I mine
green channels in it.
My body hollows spaces in its sun.
I find each line upon its sundial,
thin pieces of not-sun.
Upon its slopes I hew out light
and also baser metals.
In tidal wave the mountain sinks.
Its valleys come to whales
and coral.
My stones go down, my house, my barn,
my frogs.
My silent gentle garden snake is drowned.
North south west east refuse
to be fixed points. They move
outside me sinking shafts in common sky.
The great glass lining of the world is broken.
The light blows out through holes. Our water
goes, and something holds my heel.

Inheritance

Tenderness for my mother
who is too old,
stomach soured with losses,
pushed me to ironing this Sunday.
I want her to Will me her rose tea set
from Lake Champlain.

**Daughter's Funeral Dirge
At A Saturday Burial**
(Union Gravediggers Quit at Noon)

She is dead, thank God.
She is dead, thank the Lord.
She is really dead.
On Thursday she lay still
and someone shut her eyelids.
On Friday Brother brought her
a bright silk dress, green.
On Saturday in the Mass
they referred to her as Sister.
Alleluia went the chorus.
She is really dead.
Her name goes on the tombstone
where deceits end up as data.
The mourners being Irish
laugh and shiver time away.
She is dead and I've been cheated.
She is dead and March winds blast me.
She is dead and I've no future.
She is dead. Dead. Dead.
As a babe I wished she'd hold me.
As a child I tagged behind her.
As a woman I brought my children
to her to appraise.
She is dead and all the waiting
for the glass of her thanksgiving
proves a waiting at the table
where wine isn't served.
She is dead and goes to heaven.
She is dead and goes to hellfire.
She is dead, we took Communion,
left her coffin at the grave.
She is dead and Father wandered.
When she sent a hearse to get him
he died and left her single.

Will the gravediggers come?
She is dead, her body's wilted.
All my war to make her happy
she has clearly won by dying.
Triumphantly dead.

Visiting A Son In Java

On my balcony, not a lover
he sits uneasily in a cane chair.
We search each other across the cement
and the ghosts between us,
attending in wordy detail to their needs.
Pleading darkness he bicycles away
to his supper. Like his breakfast
it will be fish and rice.
The hotel waiter offers me wine.
I will wait but it may never happen.
The betchak drivers talk all night
idly, with soft laughter,
below my window.

The Face In The Camera

Having died he becomes more vivid.
The planes of his face emerge.
Where the camera frolicked
and was young, heedless, blurry,
death has brought grave clarity.

I am possessed by energy
of two people, one myself, one him.
Where he tossed great shovelfuls of snow
away from the path; laughing
with his brother at the morning
and the heat of his body and the visions
of breath on the air, of soft crystals
spilling through the light;

finished the path and went on to school;
I am forced to keep plying the shovel,
keep toiling up mountains,
keep checking my ropes, keep reading
about oceans, rock, stars, blood
-- any interest he might have tracked.
The face in the camera denies me
my separate choice.

The Couple

They stay as drops
of sap
on a leaf.

Angers of old age
shake them
toothless.

Each threatens
I will die
and leave you.

Cracked bells ringing
the frozen
notes.

Of Generations And Being Woman

Stuck in old Oedipal dreams
I will have a king or no one,
and know that means no one,
there are no kings about
except in heaven.
I pirouette in my white dress
when somebody turns the key
of the music box I dance on,
twirling and twirling
to the old tunes of the carp,
the prince and the peasant,
the sun and the moon,
the land and the sea.
The carp gives me three wishes,
his wishes, and the prince
ordered this lovely dress
in his pride, and the peasant
expects the same soup
his mother fed him.
The sun shines his light
on the moon. But the land
is quiet and changes little.
The best of my father,
and the best of me,
and the best of *his* father,
are silent in my dead son.
The sea comes in and goes out,
comes in and goes out,
the sea moves in silence
or with great noise
against the rock-locked
land I am.   I am.

Phantoms

The first ivory gulls to reach Seymore Island
in spring are greeted by utter desolation. Ice
fog drifting in from open water shrouds pressure
ridges piled high in the pack ice by the crushing
movements of wind and tide, and the only
evidence of the gulls' nesting places are boulders
that protrude above windswept snow.
— S.D. MacDonald, *Audubon* May 1976

The night dreams come as ivory gulls
making their long cries and yielding nothing
to present time. I am
still married and the children green
water sprouts wild with growing,
great delicate leaves on puny stems
in my dreams, in my gulls.

Sometimes I'm fifteen and sometimes fifty
but the children are young. I think they may be
mocking my life, and the man is always
without age, husband, hewer of wood
and drawer of water, a mating sculpted
by polar winds, a marriage frozen
in pressure ridges from the crushing tides.

My gulls are colors of the arctic June,
ivory on ice and the lilac linings
of their mouths. The foxes
maraud their eggs, here in the north
where everything's eaten --
even the bloodstained snow.

Our marriage lasts the midnight suns
and the months of daylong nights, in my dreams,
in my gulls with their long cries
surviving the eons, alive if as phantoms
in God's northernmost eye.

ALEXANDRA GRILIKHES

During the past five years I have become intensely interested in the sources of my work. Much of my poetry deals with the woman artist. In following that thread I discovered that for me the act of creation resembles what the Mistress of the Animals does.

The oldest deity on earth was the Great Mother and right after her came the Mistress of the Animals. A primitive, powerful figure, she was conceived of as having mastery over all wild beasts, both those outside and those within us.

I was enormously attracted by the idea that it is a female being who is strong enough to master *all* animal impulse, both inner and outer. Throughout the history of art she is there, shown as strong and female, surrounded by animals, grasping a beast in each arm or hand. That this power is female seemed not only true but *felt*. I mean felt as female by me as I have never experienced the power of any male deity.

How then is the making of art analogous to what the great goddess does? To give coherence to the animal, inner and outer, is to transform, and at least on one level, to master.

Having found the *Potnia Theron* (as the Mistress is known in Greek) to be one of the deepest sources of my work, I went deeper into my female feelings, my own myth/ history to locate my thoughts and feelings in the larger female consciousness. I experienced personal female deities -- really parts of myself -- as modes of being to which I could turn in moments of desperation. Solitude was one of these deities. I know that if I do not lose the consciousness of my female feelings I can be at one with myself no matter what is happening around me.

My poem, *Feeling The Goddess II,* reflects the early *Potnia Theron,* she who resides in our most primary feelings where there is no speech. We fear and welcome her, alternately:

> . . . . .
> knows you're afraid of her
> coming loves your fear
> finds you the path, waits
> moves on into the day of the
> world. With
> you.

The Mistress of the Animals appears also as a sophisticated and developed figure in the poem *Watching The Dance.* The viewer watches the dancers, is conscious of herself as viewer, as part creator (making the "explosion" of the work happen) is conscious of herself as viewer again. Dancer as maker and Viewer as maker mirror and feel each other intensely throughout the occurring dance.

> I
> see them through
> fire the shimmering
> faces fade in my face
> the mouth feels the curve
> of their limbs and I open them
> slowly feeling serenely excited
> closer and warmer
>   keeping my distance
>   . . . . .

Here, both watcher and dancer are coming to terms with human movement, the primary sensual basis of dance. Both are actively engaged in transforming their animal which is not only alive but crucial to all their creative acts. Without the life of the inner animal the Mistress is nothing. All the transformative powers of this goddess reside in us and it is our choice and our need to use them well.

Further Remarks

The function of poetry and the performance of poetry

Coming from my own deep sources, the poem will reach those same sources in you. The level at which I encounter myself is the level at which you will encounter yourselves.

The task of art, if art has a task, is: to transform consciousness.

The poem is restorative rather than fragmenting.

Body of words equals body. Challenges. Throws you off balance. The map is not the territory but poetry performed strives constantly in the direction of territory. Everyday experience fragments us, distorts us, distorts the body. A poem should somehow evoke the living presence of the human body. Whole.

The art of writing down signifies the splitting of mind and body. I believe that in the performance of the poem we heal the split. That the poem, having come forth from the whole person must be revealed to us by the whole person. And the person becomes the poem in uttering the poem.

In performance of the poem, the rhythms and cadences of human breathing move the performer. Listening, you move in synchrony with those rhythms and cadences, inhaling and exhaling. Moving imperceptibly in synchrony with the poet's rhythm you are totally engaged and unaware of everything else. The transaction between performer and listener is completed. That there is no separation between artist and audience is a primitive, perhaps frightening revelation.

The question arises. Which is the real poem? The poem on paper or read aloud? Is the text the score for performance? Are there as many poems as there are hearers? A voice on the airwaves. Part of the poem is where you are sitting. Unseen, the poem comes to you in your banal life as a mystery threatening to overthrow you. What do you hear coming through? The disembodied voice? Body of words equals body. The map is not the territory but poetry in its performance becomes territory from map. If the performer isn't fully engaged, is the listener? I become my words when I speak. Body of words equals body, you breathe my rhythms. My voice becomes the energy you breathe to. The level at which you meet yourself listening. No poet before you, nothing to look at, a voice coming over. Overcomes.

Watching The Dance
(For Martha Graham)

the battle before us. Walk through
enthralled. From the spine
outwards, imitate the tree.

Where is the leap from the maze?
Always the
maze with
bodies the
net wrapping up.

Brought to their knees.
Undulate. Pass
into afternoon. Unravel
the word that waits to be
formed in the mouth

       body
    in midair
breaks out in the instant
of wildness

     Who
      shrouds herself
with a quick shift
in the dark cloak upwards?
Imitate the tree. Words, the
body that's drawn from air
by the movement of will   iron
                    clad
                    moves

in the limbs
like the lioness
passes through grass
lands in sleep. Hands

shudder. Speaking. Force
air against mouth the arrogant
question. I
see them through
     fire the shimmering
faces fade in my face
the mouth feels the curve
of their limbs and I open them
slowly feeling serenely excited
closer and warmer
                    keeping my distance.
Here in the orchestra, there
on the stage, breaking
the flesh of the contract, my
love.

The Vanguard Artist Dreams Her Work

those
where our mouths
clasp and we're
overcome me continually
in the midst of important
matters
          Off in the Caribbean
          sky I'm taking a breath
          taking dive over the beautiful
          cliff and the
flower soaks through me I
fantasize terrific
longings in color
   spending it all you
   become fruit in my
veins soaking through soaking
through I
hit water
swimming for life.

The Film By The Woman

no   warning   she is
tormenting the myths that torment
you

   you, struggle in the ravaged
sky, the storm too large

            wounded where you least
wish to be wounded

               Where will you go
with it? It has always been yours
the death
or the mother

it will be yours
more and more

Potter

Between
>night and dark
>nearness and far
>sweetness and death

between
>sweetness and
>death
>nearness and
>far
>
>night and dark

her blue hands carry the great earth
cover, cut the spine of the wind

between
>moisture and deep
>the throat of the clay voice

closes
>hands   soft in the water
>slow   in the water
>blurred hands   I

shall be drawn through

curve the spine of the wind
I shall be drawn through in magic
I shall be drawn through in fever
open my hands in the sea

enter the house.

Mistress Of The Animals

you will know her presence
in the half-light
fathoming her power
you cannot see her

in the howl of animals
who make the quick
slide through the
grass, her power
in their blood
noisily beating
and echoing in the
flesh of the hunter attempting
to silence his
pounding breath, Mistress
of animals be
kind, give

succor in the dark
be sun in the
dark

Our Lady, Solitude

      was it moments like these
that made you think of her? Hunger.

elegant she is. no one knows her
name her face is seen through
mirrors an unknown
named her, her architecture a
passageway, but, too,

she is hail
maddening your face

having
known her forever
I have only just discovered
she is a great fruit
to eat in the midst of noise, passage,
the threat of being totally dis

     armed

Listening To The Story Of Your Life

Overwhelming, the torpor
of your twisted lives how you lay
back revealing your timidness all

day you had been fishing with different
baits. As you thrust your
arm over your wounded by the light eyes I

lowered the shade, gently, drank
your extended presences, took
your languidness, let it grow
momentarily for
both of us, ignored the
tangled lines, found
my hands working the lampshade
down for your wounded
eyes, slipped the
shadows deep into your garrulous
mouth
kissed you goodbye
when you least expected it;
we were both happy

Isabel Rawsthorne Standing In
A Street In Soho

The portrait by Frances Bacon

                Going and
    coming I
remain
exactly where I am
taking with me
the days
I live polluted as sky in
                I make a mandala
                of scrawled air
                encased in noises
                of pencils and

lies, clum
    siness
    my shoes
    my dear an emergency.
Outside
and in
I am all one
carrying with me
burdens you wouldn't
believe in my hair a
nest of medusas   as I'm transfixed
                in the thunderous
                raining of dogs
                my face
                the only thing to believe in
                I tell you oh
in my speech that does not
speak in my
hair that strains towards you
                like a medieval war machine

I am beautiful
in my terror my
grotesque stretched
frame you will never forget
once you have struggled awhile
in my clanking circle beauty is knowing
                    you will never forget me my
                    speckled eyes my
                    mauled body
                    in all its open shame Isabel
                    Isabel it's all I have
                    to give and I
                    don't hold it back, no

Being Driven

It was crunched out
of my life it
was my life

the throat twists
in my neck like the
twist in the road

smell of gasoline
with the cold spit glare
of the icy
roads my breath

with a hot life of its own
gets lost in the dark
car   driving

away from cities into the thing
of being alone, the road

reaches away,
from your
piano to my
house I'm
always driving
away at
night
on
roads full of ice the secret

still to the touched
to be fathomed. Then, driving to
you I was not
Driven. Now

I am.

Feeling The Goddess   II

things quietly violent
into the sun

everything moves

who flits and fixes
starts and weaves
in the tree grove, road,
overgrown woods,
paths full of stones,

she begins
in the eyes of the mountain
always descends to the sea
in her path
everything moves, twitches and
starts and falls back, shuddering

Who moves her? Waits till
she finds me? Animates my
limbs makes my hair
murmur   spits and
fixes its way into the meadow,
breaks paths, makes me lose my
way

Knowing I'm lost
wavers before me
knows I'm afraid of her
coming, loves my fear
finds me the path, waits,
moves on into the day of the
world. With
me

MAXINE SHAW

My grandmother Lucille was a writer, although she never attempted to publish anything. She had boxes and boxes of poems, and I remember her writing anti-war poetry during the Korean War, even though everyone around her supported that war.

She must have decided before I was born that I too would be a writer because some of my earliest memories are of her sitting at a typewriter while I dictated stories and poems to her.

From the very beginning she encouraged me to submit my work -- to a Mother's Cookies jingle contest when I was in the third grade (I won a walking doll), to *Jack and Jill Magazine* when I was in the fourth (my first rejection slip) and to places like *Dig Magazine* when I was a teenager. Looking back I wonder why she never had so much confidence in herself and her own poetry. . .

She and her mother raised me until I was nine years old, and both of them were strong women, used to doing things their own way. Grandma Lucille was arrested at 16 for dancing cheek to cheek, she divorced long before it was socially acceptable, and she worked and supported me and Grandma Cora. In fact, she's in her seventies and she's still working.

Grandma Cora, born in the 1860's, went to college but dropped out to elope with a plumber. Her parents found their note and chased them across Kent, Ohio in a horse and buggy, but gave up after a neighbor lied and said they were long gone. Grandma and her husband then headed for Oregon, later moving down to California where she lived to be 94, cooking from scratch, making my clothes, fixing the faucets, and telling me stories of her childhood.

Living with those two women for the first decade of my life I learned that there was nothing a woman couldn't do. It wasn't something they taught me exactly -- just something that they breathed out and I breathed in every day. There we were, the three of us, alone, without men, doing fine and of course I would go to college and of course I would be a poet and of course I would do whatever I damn well pleased.

Tengo Puerto Rico En Mi Corazón

rafael laughed when i said i was puerto rican
yet he should know that living a thing day after day
makes you part of it
the hours the days the years
one w/language culture dreams

vickie torres
my mother in new york
taught me evrything i know
about the practical side of child rearing
brought my son's fever down when he had roseola
fed me enormous dishes of arroz con algo every day
and this and only this saved me from imminent starvation

i am new yorican
my language is spanglish
i cannot speak one for any length of time w/o inserting
words or phrases of the other
cannot spell in english anymore
break things that should be ripped/
transpose sentence structure

have relived my childhood w/ nydia
pedro perez pinta pinturas
el palo en el fondo de la mar
brinca la tablita
until they are totally fused with
redlightgreenlight
mothermayi
the old lady who swallowed the fly

i know more about puerto rican history
than that of my native state
more about the tainos
than my ancestors the cherokee
like other puerto ricans
i come from a mixture of the three:

indian
black -- thru the blood of my son
spanish, catalan -- deya mallorca -- 1970

my alias ann (anita) bosch, a true representation of me
bosch, recognized as spanish if you are,
taken for anglo if you are not

felt so strange answering the questionnaire in the clinic today
are you of spanish american origin?
i know my forefathers came from england, germany, oklahoma
but it would be denying my roots to say no

Ballad Of The Two Grandfathers
by Nicolas Guillen
(Translated for Wamwega Christopher Shaw)

Shadows that only I can see,
my two grandfathers guard me.

Bone-tipped lance,
drum of tanned hide and wood:
my black grandfather.
Wide-necked ruff,
grey war armor:
my white grandfather.

Africa of humid jungles
and great stilled drums. . .
"I'm dying!"
(Says my black grandfather.)
Dark alligator waters,
green coconut mornings. . .
"I'm tired!"
(Says my white grandfather.)
Sails of bitter wind,
galleon gleaming with gold. . .
"I'm dying!"
(Says my black grandfather.)
The virgin neck of the seaboard
seduced by glass beads. . .

"I'm tired!"
(Says my white grandfather.)
Twenty four carat sun hammered into relief,
imprisoned in the rim of the tropics;
moon round and clean above the sleep of monkeys!

So many ships! So many ships!
So many blacks! So many blacks!
The long brilliance of the sugar cane!
The whip the master holds!
Stone of blood and weeping,
veins and eyes half open,
and empty dawns
and afternoons of sugar mills,
and a great voice, a strong voice
tearing apart the silence.
So many ships! So many ships!
So many blacks!
Shadows that only I can see,
my two grandfathers guard me.

Don Federico shouts to me,
and Papa Facundo is silent;
at night they both dream,
and walk and walk.
I bring them together.
            — Federico!
Facundo! They embrace.
They sigh together. They
lift up their strong heads,
both the same size,
below distant stars
black anguish and white anguish;
both the same size,
shouting, dreaming, crying, singing.
Dreaming, crying, singing.
Crying, singing.
Singing!

Sensemayá: Chant For The Killing Of A Snake

by Nicolas Guillen
translated by Maxine Shaw

¡Mayombe-bombe-mayombé!
¡Mayombe-bombe-mayombé!
¡Mayombe-bombe-mayombé!

The snake has glass eyes;
the snake comes and wraps himself around a stick;
with glass eyes, around a stick,
with glass eyes.
The snake walks without feet;
the snake hides in the grass;
walking he hides in the grass
walking with no feet

¡Mayombe-bombe-mayombé!
¡Mayombe-bombe-mayombé!
¡Mayombe-bombe-mayombé!

You hit him with the hatchet and he dies:
¡hit him now!
Don't hit him with your feet, he will bite you!
don't hit him with your feet, he will go!

Sensemaya, la culebra,
sensemaya.
Sensemaya, with his eyes,
sensemaya.
Sensemaya, with his tongue,
sensemaya.
Sensemaya, with his mouth,
sensemaya.

The dead snake cannot eat;
the dead snake cannot hiss;
cannot walk,
cannot run.

The dead snake cannot see;
cannot drink;
cannot breathe
i cannot bite!

¡Mayombe-bombe-mayombé!
Sensemaya, la culebra. . .
¡Mayombe-bombe-mayombé!
Sensemaya, does not move. . .
¡Mayombe-bombe-mayombé!
Sensemaya, la culebra. . .
¡Mayombe-bombe-mayombé!
¡Sensemaya, he's dead!

For Mrs. W, Who Would Not Be Black, White Or Other

in my grandmother's day they would have called us
halfbreeds, mulattos or niggerlovers
by blood or by love embracing two cultures
never embraced by either one

today they asked you to choose, any one but only one,
each moving to separate corners
and you sat, dazed, in the middle of the room trying
to make them understand

i wanted to sit with you
apart from all of them
and their demands that we reject parts of ourselves
i wanted to cry with you
to tell you that behind my blond hair
is a cherokee grandmother and my father who rejected her
that behind my blue eyes is a black son
and a black lover who won't introduce me to his family

i wanted to tell you that i too am too pale
for the black parents council
and dark enough that my mother's last words were
"no nigger's any grandson of mine"

i wanted to tell you that i too
cannot divide the blood
that flows through my heart
when asked my race i want to mark all
or none
or even just human
but mrs. w, there is no box for that
there is no box for us

Going Back To School

the professor is a magician
he makes me disappear and performs for younger women
he is my age and balding, but they do not notice
they laugh at his sleight of word
he pulls an innuendo from his pants/ they applaud
he takes a drug reference from his nose/ they cheer
he tells them they know nothing and begins with simple mathematics
i tell him i know calculus, but i am still invisible
i leave the room shouting
no one hears
they are measuring his cock

i take refuge in another classroom
the prof is a woman and i smile
she looks familiar
she is Sister Mary First Grade Teacher
i remember that she has favorites
that she likes the smart ones
i am smart, so i smile at her
but she blesses her doctoral candidates
and i am still invisible

Issue

a non-negotiable issue for both of us
    my child exists
    we hear his breathing in the other room
    he will knock on our door in the morning

i understand
    you have torn out your roots
    your parents are dead
    your ex-wife less than a memory
    the son you reared on weekends is grown
    a name on an infrequent letter

understand
    i can name the branches on my family tree
    for the past nine centuries
    my grandmother's picture dominates my parlor
    i wear her rose beads

we understand, both of us
that we love each other
we see it reflected in the tears
that have discolored our faces
tonight, more than any night
we feel it in the violence
as our bodies meet

        i love you/ you love me
        but i am a mother
        you will not be a father
        the issue is children
        and the issue is not negotiable

Damaris

named for a circus performer
who dropped from the high wire
as you dropped from the belly of your mother
for damaris, whose blood burst onto the sand
damaris, life from death

damaris, you are 24 years old and have eight children
you are beautiful, but your teeth are rotten
you are beautiful, but the veins in your legs are as thick as pencils

damaris, i love your daughter
i love her as the daughter i will never have
i would steal her from you
she would never have eight children
she would be a dentist
her legs would stay young and firm

i would take her from you, but she would never be mine
her name is your name
her face in the mirror is your face
she would sleep in my house but you
would visit her in my dreams
each night growing older and greyer
you would wear black stockings
but they could never cover your legs
in the morning, always
there would be blood on the floor

For Billie Holiday And Janis Joplin

Lady. . .
Janis. . .
i never rode no horse like you
but i know enof
about another white powder
to understand
what kept them heavy, heavy blues
from killing you all at once
evry time you screamed em out

oh, yeah, know how to paint
a mask on my face
powder my nose and smile
shout loneliness despair
in a poem
like you wailed yrs out in a song

know how to take the pieces of this jigsaw puzzle life
fill in the missing ones with a beautiful white powder
inhale illusions of love and success
or paint them on yr arm
its all the same
the man beside you loves you really loves you
the public really loves you
if you paint it that way

and you never wanna come down
sleepless, rockin in yr chair
blues beginnin to hurt again

so you get back up there and ride on
and on and on
till the pain
finally
breaks thru the powder
and kills you anyway

evrybody say you died of an overdose
but me and my nose
we know
it kept you alive
for a long
long time

JAN CLAUSEN

Early influences: the nuclear family; redwood trees; air raid drills; books; suburbs; the Cascade Mountains of the Pacific Northwest; Bob Dylan; the drug culture; various male lovers; the rarified atmosphere of a "fine small liberal arts college" (which I fled after three years); Portland, Oregon; the Left, especially after 1970; assorted shit jobs.

I began writing in high school, secretly and in great isolation. The process of training myself to write and of establishing my identity as a "real" writer in both my own and the world's eyes has been a long one. It's still difficult for me to accept the fumbling, the failures, the intermittent silences that seem to be an inevitable part of writing. And I've never gotten used to boldly identifying myself as a writer when some new acquaintance comes out with the inevitable, "What do you *do*?" (especially since the standard follow-up is, "But can you make a living that way?").

For me, becoming a writer has been closely connected with coming out as a lesbian. Both processes necessitated making a major break with standard assumptions about who I would be and what I would do in my life; both accelerated significantly when I moved from Portland to New York in 1973. I then found that I was much more interested in writing about imaginary relationships between women than in writing about my actual relationship with a man. I joined a writing support group which ended up supporting not only my writing but my decision to come out. I now feel myself a part of a recent but already clearly delineated tradition of women writing primarily for other women and speaking directly from their experience. I participate in a loosely-knit but remarkably energetic community of women writing, many of whom publish their own work.

I am still struggling to define to my own satisfaction the relationship between my writing and my politics. I do not believe that any of us writes in a vacuum; for me, there is a clear connection between the sharpened awareness of the world that writing entails and a recognition of the need for social/ political change. I see my own writing as political, not only in terms of content but in terms of the audience I address and the publishing decisions I make. Yet there is too much that words cannot do. I'm painfully conscious of the failure of any existing political movement to effectively challenge the race/sex/class structure of our society, of my own failure to identify adequate avenues of political action.

I live in Brooklyn, New York with my lover and her child. My economic existence continues to be marginal -- unemployment, typing jobs, etc. I write as much as possible, poetry and increasingly more fiction and critical prose. Three friends and I collectively edit *Conditions,* a magazine of women's writing.

Scenario

in this one
you're the woman
i'm the man

and what i despise

is your bourgeois taste in clothes

and how, when i cry
you rush to comfort me
as if my pain
weren't wiser than your kiss

and the scrubbed, unblemished
porcelain of your sink

and the softness of your skin

Waking At The Bottom Of The Dark

waking
at the bottom of the dark
to the love of your body
to drink cold tea
and stuff clothes in a sack
and help the sleepy child
with her difficult socks
i think of wartime
an evacuation

but you're only off
for a weekend in the country
and it is good
to be out walking early
a day so cold like this
drawn striped with clouds

although i suppose
the park is dangerous
there are old men walking dogs
there are thin young men
hunched down in their thin jackets
i am the only woman

yes i am the woman
whom personal happiness wraps
a magic coat
the windows are glazed with light
the trees shake out
their final green and gold
above the leaf-thick grass
the meadow opens, spacious
as a prairie

oh how can i remember

*it was winter. clear. the light
was shining through the crystal
park.*

Upstate

country woman

cards

slit
gypsy eyes

bi
sexual

that knife
beneath your skirt

the transplant

the plants
reach out new hands
toward the light

the cats adjust
the landlord's •
satisfied

it seems only i
wake daily
to discover

this un-
accustomed fact
of our joined lives

indelible as
a scar
a newborn baby

uneasily present
like a heart
or kidney

the body
has not yet
accepted

grandma

for fifty years
his breathing at my back
then separate rooms
and then his blindness
terror of the dark
then even that light gone

i visit his body
in the nursing home
i clean this house
and hope for another summer
a few tomatoes

the amputation
arrives almost too late

my children come
heavy with money
and middle age
complaining of daughters
who refuse to marry

but more and more
i want to be alone

sometimes i remember
a winter i taught school
in a border district
it was before the war

there were nights i walked
the path, the icebound river
miles from the nearest farm
unafraid, wolves howling
on the frozen shore

the kitchen window

1.

in Bohack
a woman my age,
kids in a stroller,
is buying mayonnaise
and chocolate bars

another woman,
maybe sixty,
talks and talks
as she waits
at an empty counter

"it's a secret.
no one's saying
a goddamned thing.
what's your number?
where can i go
to get some service?"

the checker
checks

2.

i don't know anything
about the pain

labor

years/ afternoons
raising kids

old hits
on the radio
dishes, diapers, mopping

the trash-filled yard
beneath the kitchen window
where trees
are going to
get rich quick and
bloom

i can't guess
the checker's
peculiar weariness,
which muscle
aches the most
with all that standing

i read Tillie Olsen
on the thirties

over and over
i try to imagine
my mother

3.

you show me the ring,
the date incised in gold,
the curled-up snapshots,
clothes to be given away:
high heels in a closet,
garter belt in a drawer

"transcendentalist periodicals,"
"shakespeare's morphology,"
your grad school papers

the child
now learning to read
came out of your body

4.

"when you and me and mommy
live together,"

Anna tells me, "you
can be the daddy,
because when you play house
you need a mommy
and a daddy."

5.

and what will we do
together
in this place
with its tile,
its aqua kitchen,
back yard
concreted over

the suburbs
yawn in my genes
like inherited cancer

i'm left
with a love for/
horror of
formica

6.

we pioneer
this life. like
pulling teeth.

weeks when
sleep recedes,
spring, everything
healing or green,

the river under
thirty feet of rock.

there's no
outwitting pain.

mother,
anaesthetized
when i was born,

was there something,
once, you
passionately wanted?

is that
the secret?

7.

Anna, fierce
in her will
to control the kittens:

I want them to eat
and
now I want them to sleep

my mother
holed up in her
crazy '50's faith

that raising children's
some sort of
sculptural art

a lifetime, whispering
white
is the color
of culture

but weeds split
the pavement

the world
cannot be saved

the whites
will be driven
at last
from Africa

8.

no words, you say

we slip
through the nets
of speech

mother, lover, friend

9.

rain on the roof

i stroke the shape of your head
the soft hair snags
it tears my cold-cracked fingers

beneath, the living roots

all night you hold me
on and on we fly
into the storm

10.

how is it possible

space
around a life

for poems
for cats
for children

Hiroshima
five years before my birth

i'm baking bread
it's twelve degrees outside

green plant on the washer
sun through the kitchen window

Poem On The Occasion Of Not Receiving
The Academy Of American Poets'
Walt Whitman Award For
An Outstanding First Manuscript Of Poetry

so a book didn't fall on you
out of the sky like a bomb,
making it easy, blotting you out,
rescuing you from the onerous chore
of functioning in your human capacity;

so a particular woman didn't fall,
ripe-plum-like, wanting, into your open lap;

so you have to go on
being fucked-up, messy, and making choices
about whom to sleep with and have
for friends and all that,
and placing words on a page one after the other,
and diverting yourself from public catastrophes
with private ones, and vice versa,
and earning a living;

and it's fine and you're restless
after work so you run
a ways in the park, because if you're not
going to be a famous poet you might as well
hang on to your body;

and two young men in full-length coats are
   tinkering
with a 50's model powder-blue buick sedan;

and the kids are tearing up and down the block
with their toys, their outdoors voices;

and on this day the people seem looser, louder;
they're looking out their windows;
your first spring on this street
and today you're not afraid
you look anglo, funky, silly, different;

"dirty lezzie," your rough cracked boots
running up those steps;

and yesterday somebody gave you
begonia cuttings, already half-rooted,
they sit there waiting in the chipped brown
   pitcher
(might as well nurture the plants
if you've got to keep living);

and sunday afternoon you got it together
to clean a bit
so now the toilet returns its pristine wink
of porcelain white each time you lift the lid;

and even if the phone never rings
you can pick it up dial it;

and you can make choices;

and find you even feel like trying to write,
competing with knocking pipes and electric
   noise
from the floor above;

(and it isn't always like this,
the poems in the cracks, how they happen,
the subway delays);

and life is slowly --

slow as the time it takes to think
any new thought; to change, cell by cell,
your whole skin --

reshaping itself, asserting cleaner edges:

slight blades of grass that can really cut,
small teeth erupting through the swollen gum.

CONTRIBUTOR NOTES

Kate Ellen Braverman lives in Los Angeles, California where she has taught poetry at the U.C.L.A. Extension, worked with the Poets-in-Schools program, and done a book review show for radio. Her poetry has appeared in a number of places, including *Bachy* (which she has edited). Harper & Row will be publishing her novel *Lithium for Medea* as well as a volume of her poetry. She is 28, and received her B.A. in Anthropology from U.C. Berkeley.

Jan Clausen lives in Brooklyn, home of Out & Out Books, a new feminist poetry press, which published her first book, *After Touch* in 1975. ($2.00 plus .50 postage and handling, 476 2nd Street, Brooklyn, NY, 11215) For information on *Conditions*, write to Conditions, c/o Klepfisz, P.O. Box 56, Van Brunt Station, Brooklyn, NY 11215.

Miriam Dyak was born in New York City on April 24, 1946— Sagittarius rising and moon in Aquarius. She grew up in Greece and Missouri, attended Oberlin College, teaches, with Poets-in-Schools, and courses in yoga, healing herbs, Womancraft. *Dying* will be published by New Victoria Publishers.

Virginia Gilbert was born in Elgin, Illinois in 1946. She has taught high school in Korea, and has taught writing and composition at the University of Utah. Poems published in *Southern Poetry Review, Crazy Horse, Poetry Now, New Voices in American Poetry: An Anthology,* and others. She received her MFA in writing from Iowa in

1971, and was awarded a National Endowment for the Arts Creative Writing Fellowship in 1976. She is living in Iran.

Alexandra Grilikhes' books are available from Woodbine Press, Providence, R.I. and New York Folder Editions. She teaches an evening workshop at the Philadelphia College of the Performing Arts and is director of the University of Pennsylvania's School of Communications library.

Elizabeth Keeler's poetry was anthologized by Peace and Pieces Foundation, along with Nellie Mill and David Hoag, in *Astrolabes* (1975). The same press also published her small chapbook *Ending Quartet.* She attended the New School for Social Research, the University of Denver and San Francisco State. "I was born in New York State but lived for twenty years in Connecticut after my parents refused to let me go West (to the edge of the earth) to college. I'm still amazed at living where mountains and sea are in the same place, and at being a good psychotherapist. But my *other* life is as a poet-farmer, presiding over a roomy backyard where my horse eats the plums as they ripen and allows me to sit on his stable ledge to write."

Rachel Maines is executive director of the Center for the History of American Needlework, a feminist foundation housed in a storefront in Pittsburgh. Her poems have been published in *Off Our Backs, Women: A Journal of Liberation,* and *Hanging Loose.* Currently, when not teaching needlework history at the University of Pittsburgh, she is helping to organize a nationwide boycott of J. P. Stevens, world's largest textile firm and notorious racist and sexist institution.

Felice Newman is a recent graduate of the University of Pittsburgh (writing and women studies) where she was nominated for a Rhodes Scholarship. She has published poems (or will shortly) in *Liberation Magazine, Amazon Poetry: An Anthology, Best Friends, Gravida,* and *Street Cries* (awards issue). She has lived in Pittsburgh for nearly ten years (and is leaving), spent quite a bit of energy working with the women's movement there.

Susan North was born in the desert and remains there. She lives with her animals and her son, resists incarceration, crowds, accreditation, and compulsive gambling with varying degrees of success. She raises dogs and blackbirds, studies French, and walks a lot. She is the author of *All That Is Left* (poems), Desert First Works.

Maxine Shaw was born in Long Beach, California in 1945, and brought up by her maternal grandmother and great grandmother. Her father was from Oklahoma, and her paternal grandmother—whom she never met—was a Cherokee. She now lives in Boston with her ten year old son and works as a bilingual teacher. Her first book of poems, *Walking Backwards Down the Kenya Coast,* was published in Milwaukee in 1970. Her second book, *Beautiful Cages,* was published in 1974 by Stone Soup Poetry, Boston. Nicòlas Guillen, the poet whose work Maxine Shaw has translated here, was named National Poet of Cuba in 1961, and is president of the Union of Cuban Writers and Artists.

Dona Stein has published poems in quite a few magazines, including *Dark Horse, Moving Out, The New York Quarterly, Women/Poems, Hollow Spring Review, Sunbury* and *Zeugma.* She recently received a Massachusetts Arts and Humanities Foundation Poetry Fellowship and is employed by Fitchburg State College.

Beverly Tanenhaus writes feminist literary criticism and poetry. She is the Director of the Women's Writing Workshop at Hartwick College, Oneonta, NY.

Mary Winfrey has published poems in *Sister,* the *Second Wave, MSS, Figs and Thistles* and the *New York Daily News.* She has degrees from Butler University and the University of Tennessee, has done additional graduate work in American Literature at the University of Wisconsin. She has taught, worked as a life guard, social worker, and editorial assistant. She is the mother of three daughters, one of whom died in 1975 of leukemia.

ACKNOWLEDGMENTS

Kate Ellen Braverman: "My Husband Who Is Not My Husband" and "Picking Up Your Mail" appeared in *Momentum* # 3, "Soon" and "7 PM" in *Ironwood* # 6, "Details" in *Rapport* #9, "Job Interview" in *Paris Review* # 64, and "Weekend Man" in *Invisible City*, July 1976. "Lies," among others of the poems in this volume, is included in *Milk Run*, Momentum Press, copyright Kate Ellen Braverman 1977.

Jan Clausen: "Scenario," "Upstate" and "Poem On The Occasion Of Not Receiving The Academy Of American Poets' Walt Whitman Award For An Outstanding First Manuscript Of Poetry" are from *After Touch*, Out & Out Books, Inc., copyright 1975 Jan Clausen. "Scenario" originally appeared in the *Village Voice.* "Grandma" appeared in the *Greenfield Review*, and "Transplant" in the *Cottonwood Review.*

Miriam Dyak: "On Having To Go Round The Circle And State Our Philosophies" originally appeared in the *Second Wave;* this poem, along with "Three" and "Forbidden Sweets" are included in *Fire Under The Water*, New Victoria Publishers, 1977. *Dying*, in excerpt here, is also published by New Victoria Publishers.

Virginia Gilbert: "Leaving, The Sepulchre City" appeared in the *Beloit Poetry Journal.*

Alexandra Grilikhes: "The Vanguard Artist Dreams Her Work" appeared in *13th Moon*, Vol. II, 2 & III, 1, Winter 1975. With a different title and in slightly different form, it originally appeared in *The Painted Bride Quarterly*, along with "Listening To The Story Of Your Life," "Potter," under the title "Forms of Clay," appeared in the *En Passant Poetry Quarterly*, #2, 1976. "Mistress Of The Animals" and "Our Lady, Solitude" are from *Aphra*, vol. 4, no. 3, 1973. "Feeling The Goddess II" under the title "XVI" is from *Sea Agon*, The Woodbine Press, 1976. "Isabel Rawsthorne Standing In A Street In Soho" is from the book of the same name, New York Folder Editions, copyright Alexandra Grilikhes, 1972. "Being Driven" appeared in *Light: A Poetry Review*, vol. 1, no. 1. "Watching The Dance" appeared in *Feminist Studies.*

Elizabeth Keeler: "Looking For Light And Finding The Sea" appeared in *Mariner* and *Gallimaufry* in 1973, "Visiting A Son In Java" in *Gypsy Table.* Many of these poems are included in *Astrolabes*, a three-poet anthology from Peace and Pieces Foundation. "Again Flowering" and "Daughter's Funeral Dirge" are from a supplementary chapbook to *Astrolabes, Ending Quartet,* copyright Elizabeth Keeler, 1975

Rachel Maines: "Textile Women" and "the tyer-in" appeared in *Women: A Journal of Liberation,* copyright 1975 by *Women: A Journal of Liberation,* 3028 Greenmount Avenue, Baltimore, Md. 21218. "Union Educator" and "Schraffts" appeared in *Speak Out,* Fall 1975, and "almost newyork" in *Riata,* Spring 1970.

Susan North: "Poem For Her Thirty-fifth Birthday" appeared in *Blue Moon News,* "There Is A Point" in *Do It Now,* "After Ten Years," "When Your Husband Goes To Prison," "Farmer's Almanac" and "Small Poem For Michael" in *Mazagine.* "For Michael" is from *All That Is Left,* Desert First Works, 1976.

Maxine Shaw: "For Mrs. W. " appeared in the *100 Flowers Anthology,* "Tengo Puerto Rico En Mi Corazon" and "For Billie Holiday and Janis Joplin" in *Beautiful Cages,* Stone Soup Poetry, copyright 1974 Maxine Shaw. "Ballad of the Two Grandfathers" appeared in *Hanging Loose,* and along with "Sensemaya" on *Black Box,* copyright 1975, New Classroom for Audio Production. Their originals, by Nicolas Guillen, appeared in 1934 in *West Indies Ltd.* "Issue" appeared in *Gravida.*

Dona Stein: "For F.J.L.," "In The Year Of The Tiger" and "Visiting M. in The Happy Valley Nursing Home" appeared in the *Hollow Spring Review,* December 1975, "Putting Mother By" in *Ploughshares,* vol. 3, no. 3 & 4, 1977, "Lady and the Wolf" in *Bosarts,* January 1975, "Van Gogh, Painting His Way Out Of The Asylum" in the *Denver Quarterly,* and "Night Garden, With Ladies" in the *Washout Review,* vol. 2, no. 3. Many of these poems are from *Children Of The Mafiosi,* West End Press, 1977.

Beverly Tanenhaus: "My Hair Is Black" appeared in *Women Writing,* February 1975.

Mary Winfrey: "Kleis," "Thoughts About Clara Schumann," "Gertrude Ederle Swims The Channel," "Historical Footnote", and "Demeter's Song" appeared in the *Second Wave.* "Hera Of The Locker Room" and "The Conditioning" appeared in *Sister.* "At Menopause" appeared in *Women: A Journal Of Liberation,* copyright 1977, *Women: A Journal Of Liberation* 3028 Greenmount Ave., Baltimore, Md. 21218.

PHOTO CREDITS

RACHEL MAINES—Lynne Stebbins Reilly, *Homestead Daily Messenger*/DONA STEIN—Valerie Grant/KATE BRAVERMAN—R. Bradley/MAXINE SHAW—Kathleen Edwards/FELICE NEWMAN—Lynn Johnson/JAN CLAUSEN—Barbara Adams/BEVERLY TANENHAUS—Barbara Adams/ALEXANDRA GRILIKHES—Stella Snead.